D1809158

The Wilderness Chef

The Wilderness Chef

The Art and Craft of One-Pan Lightweight Trail Cooking

John R. Weber

Writer's Showcase

San Jose New York Lincoln Shanghai

The Wilderness Chef
The Art and Craft of One-Pan Lightweight Trail Cooking

All Rights Reserved © 2002 by John R. Weber

No part of this book may be reproduced or transmitted in any form or by any means, graphic, electronic, or mechanical, including photocopying, recording, taping, or by any information storage retrieval system, without the permission in writing from the publisher.

Writer's Showcase
an imprint of iUniverse, Inc.

For information address:
iUniverse, Inc.
5220 S. 16th St., Suite 200
Lincoln, NE 68512
www.iuniverse.com

ISBN: 0-595-21505-X

Printed in the United States of America

Dedication

"It is not enough to fight for the land; it is even more important to enjoy it. While you can. While it is still there. So get out there and mess around with your friends, ramble out yonder and explore the forests, encounter the grizz, climb the mountains. Run the rivers, breathe deep of that yet sweet and lucid air, sit quietly for a while and contemplate the precious stillness, that lovely, mysterious and awesome space."

Edward Abbey

This volume of the Wilderness Chef is fondly dedicated to the unique creativity of the poetry of Shel Silverstein (1930-1999). Friends and I have spent much time together around campfires with his poems in quiet contemplation of the precious stillness, in that lovely, mysterious and awesome space.

A Campfire with Friends

There is something magical about a campfire. Night presses in from all sides but it's held at bay by the fire's glow while we watch incandescent figures dance in the flames. Outside the circle of light, lurk all sorts of fairies and strange creatures. The unblinking eye of the moon stares down at us and illuminates the naked tree limbs that stretch out like white-bleached arms to grasp at passersby. But in our circle of friendship gathered about the fire, all are safe; all are warm. We face inward toward the firelight, and shoulder to shoulder, we boldly turn our backs on the mysteries and fears hidden in the dark.

Come! Come join our circle and share tales and poems best told by campfire light. But be warned! As the sun rises, the magic will disappear with the dark. For in bright morning all that will remain of our fiery fellowship this night will be ashes and memories. Shel, you will be missed.

John Weber

Contents

Introduction

"All these things here collected are not mine,
But diverse grapes make but one sort of wine;
So I, from many learned authors took
The various matters printed in this book…
…Some things are very good, pick out the best,
Good wits compiled them and I wrote the rest.
If thou dost buy it, it will quit thy cost,
Read it and all thy labour is not lost."

John Taylor

What kind of a wilderness chef are you? At one extreme is the Gourmet. You're probably a Gourmet Chef if you delight in preparing complex meals that require long lists of ingredients, a tinker's horde of pots and pans for preparation and an ocean of hot water for cleanup. The Gourmet Chef hikes or paddles only to occupy time from one meal to the next so another elaborate recipe can be executed to please taste buds of companions.

At the other extreme is the Spartan. You might be a Spartan Chef if you don't want to be bothered with the niceties of preparing meals. Meal planning is done with a formula: Count the number of meals required, multiply by the number in the party, divide by two and buy that many packages each of macaroni and cheese and Ramen noodles (a variety of flavors). Toss in a dozen day-old bagels, a box of tea bags and supplies are ready for a weekend trip*. A Spartan Chef considers that time spent preparing meals would be better used hiking, paddling, or exploring and photographing the outdoors.

---

* A friend of mine, a dedicated Spartan, volunteered to take care of meals for a weekend trip and this is *exactly* how she did it. I generously offered to take over the chore next trip.

This collection of outdoor recipes and cooking techniques is the middle ground between the extremes of the Gourmet and the Spartan Chefs. The recipes are designed to be easy and quick to prepare using one pan on a single burner stove. They are made from inexpensive ingredients available at most supermarkets to satisfy the Spartan chef and yet have the taste, texture and appeal of fine food for the Gourmet chef. Also, most of the preparation of the meal is done at home, reducing the effort required in camp.

Goals of wilderness cooking:

The Spartan views meal preparation as a necessary task to finish as quickly and easily as possible. The Gourmet thinks it's an elaborate production requiring lots of time and effort. Both are wrong! Wilderness meals should be:

- **Fun:** Preparing meals should not be drudgery. Planning menus, selecting foods, pre-trip preparation and cooking the final meal can be extremely satisfying.

- **Not particularly precise:** Following the recipe exactly will produce a good meal, but precision is not required. Recipes are designed to allow for leeway in measuring. As long as ingredients are measured reasonably close, most meals will turn out well—or at least edible.

- **Easy to prepare in camp:** After a long day hiking, canoeing, or backpacking, a good meal of quality food is uppermost on everyone's mind. However, no one wants to use dwindling energy to prepare an elaborate meal. Recipes in this collection have been designed for easy preparation.

- **Made from easy-to-find ingredients:** Ingredients, with one significant exception discussed later, are available in most medium to large grocery stores.

- **Inexpensive:** There are no expensive freeze-dried or commercially prepared outdoor foods in any of the recipes. A trail meal should cost about what a meal at home would cost.

- **Of sufficient quantity:** The portions in many commercial light-weight foods simply do not have enough calories and nutrition to fuel someone engaged in the hard labor of wilderness travel. The portions in most recipes are large enough for the biggest appetites.

- **Imaginative:** Some recipes use foods prepared in unlikely combinations and in unusual ways. Variations on the basic recipe are included with every recipe. Invent variations for each recipe; experimenting is part of the fun.

- **Eclectic:** Foods selected from disparate sources are used to create meals with a wide range of taste, texture and color to prevent the meal doldrums that can appear on long trips.

- **Prepared with flair:** Quality meals prepared with care and attention to detail reflect the positive attitude of the chef toward his or her craft and companions.

- **Satisfying physically and mentally:** Mealtime is more than an opportunity to renew energy sources. It's a chance to kick back and relax several times a day and savor a satisfying meal with friends as part of the overall outdoor experience.

- **Easy to clean up:** Meals should be designed to minimize cleanup. This will reduce the time required for this chore and limit the environmental impact of cooking.

Using a combination of inexpensive grocery store foods, cooking tools such as the Outback Oven, textured vegetable protein and some imagination, the wilderness chef can prepare meals on a wilderness trip that are highlights of the day.

All recipes have been prepared successfully* many times on the trail in all weather by people from preteen (youth group members mostly) to adults with a wide range of cooking experience and skill. However, no matter how simple preparation seems to be, any new recipe should be prepared at home at least once before taking it on the trail. Experimenting with new recipes in camp when meals and morale are at stake is a bad idea, especially if tired, hungry companions outnumber the chef.

"Cooking—like anything—must be fun and not taken too seriously."
Ferdinand Metz, President, The Culinary Institute of America

---

* Well, maybe the 'meatless' meatloaf recipe wasn't all that successful, but that batch of brownies was not my fault.

-One-

The Cooking Equipment

The Basic Kitchen

> He carried his snowshoes and a blanket…on his back, and I carried the provisions—smoked eels and cold grease—enough for three days.
>
> Willa Cather, *Shadows on the Rock*

Wilderness cooking requires that someone carry the kitchen: Stove, fuel, pans, chef's tools and food. The chef needs all the equipment required to prepare a meal, but at the same time, it must be as light as possible. Fortunately these two requirements are not mutually exclusive. The load can be reduced significantly by carefully selecting equipment and food.

Stove:

When I started backpacking there were few choices of stoves. I started with a *Svea* 123 stove[*] and for years successfully prepared hundreds of meals in spite of its limitations. Today, there are a large number of stoves on the market with many features including those that burn a variety of

---

[*] After more than 30 years, I still use this stove. Would that I get that kind of service from the new stoves I purchased over the last few years.

fuels. The inexperienced chef should research the different types of stoves and test a variety before actually using one away from home.

Stoves are classified according to the type of fuel they burn: liquid fuel or canister. Each type of stove has advantages and disadvantages discussed in detail in the references at the beginning of Appendix III. I prefer liquid fuel stoves to canister types. Whichever stove is used, the chef should practice conservation to reduce the amount of fuel needed to prepare a meal. Lower fuel consumption means less weight, less use of fossil fuels and less cost.

Fuel saver tips:

- **Prepare food first**: Read the recipe carefully and do as much food preparation as possible before lighting the stove.

- **Use the most efficient cooking equipment**: Preparing a meal in the Outback Oven, for example, uses far less fuel than preparing the same meal in an open pan.

- **Use a single stove**: Learn to prepare meals using only one stove.

- **Use a windscreen**: Even a small breeze can carry significant amounts of heat away from the stove. Use an aluminum windscreen or even a pan turned on its side to block the wind.

- **Use the correct pan size**: A small pan requires less heat than a large pan to prepare the same meal.

- **Use lids**: Tight-fitting lids trap heat, significantly reducing the amount of fuel needed to bring foods to a boil.

- **Never boil when simmering will do**: Adjust the flame as low as possible to get as much heat as needed, but no more. If food is to be simmered, boiling will not necessarily decrease cooking time.

- **Use heat exchangers**: A heat exchanger is a metal baffle that wraps around a pan and captures some of the heat from the stove that would normally escape around the sides of the pan and transfers it to the pan.

- **Never leave stoves unattended**: Monitor a stove constantly for safety reasons and to save fuel by regulating the flame.
- **Turn off the stove before a meal is completely done**: It's not necessary to heat food until it's fully cooked. Once the food has come to a boil and it's almost done, the stove can be turned off and the food will continue to cook 5 to 10 minutes, depending on the weather.
- **Don't spill liquid fuel**: Refuel stoves carefully using a funnel to avoid spillage and reduce the danger of fire and injury.
- **Stack pans**: Buy pan sets that will stack. By using a pan containing another course of the meal as a lid, the heat from the pan below will keep the food in the other pan warm while preparing the next course.
- **Use a water filter instead of boiling water**: Boiling will purify water, but it takes a lot of fuel, especially in cold weather. Use a water filter to purify the water supply.
- **Limit use of hot water**: Use only as much hot water as required for cleanup. Since most of the recipes use a meat substitute, there is no grease to clean and hot water is often not necessary.

Open Fires: yea or nay?

"Traditional camp scenes were pungent with wood smoke. The sounds of a crackling fire and kindling being chopped were the auditory background. The stew pot hung from a wire or rested on a metal grill set above the fire and after dinner, the flames warmed the group as stars appeared and the night noises in the forest came alive."

Alan S. Kesselheim

"A source of much misery in old-fashioned camping was the campfire…The camp cook was frequently pictured as a tranquil man hunkered down by a bed of glowing coals, turning plump trout in the frying pan with the blade of his hunting knife. In reality, the camp cook was a wildly distraught individual who charged through waves of heat and speared savagely with a long sharp stick at a burning hunk of meat he had tossed on the grill from a distance of twenty feet…The smoke always blew directly into the eyes of the campers. No one minded much since it prevented you from seeing what you were eating."

Patrick F. McManus, outdoor humor writer

Memories of open fires tend to be fickle. My experiences with open fires seem to parallel those of McManus. Whichever experience you remember, there is considerable debate about using stoves or building open fires in the backcountry. Not from me, however. I am irrevocably anti-open fire. Anywhere other than in a developed car campsite with permanent fire pits, an open fire is only for emergencies. Reasons for not building open fires fall into two areas of concern:

General issues:

- **Wildfires:** Open fires create a risk of starting wildfires.
- **Water:** Extra water, sometimes in short supply, is required to extinguish a fire.
- **Soil damage:** Intense heat from a fire will sterilize soil beneath it.
- **Blackened rock surfaces:** Built on rock, fires blacken surfaces, leaving evidence of man's use.
- **Wildlife:** Animals will be attracted to open fire areas where food was prepared.
- **Wood use:** Fires consume wood that would otherwise decompose and improve soil.
- **Appearance:** Trees stripped of dead branches have an unattractive, unnatural appearance.

- **Fire rings**: Old rock fire rings invite others to use the same area, causing additional damage.
- **Fire scars**: Fragile areas in extremely high or dry areas will show fire scars for decades.
- **Cleanup**: Fire sites are dirty and require time to cleanup and restore the area to a natural state.
- **Trash burning**: There is a temptation to burn trash in an open fire instead of carrying it out (Just a little won't hurt just this once.).
- **Spark damage**: Get too close and the fire will melt man-made fabrics and sparks will melt holes in tents.

Cooking issues:

- **Availability of fuel**: Dry wood can't always be found. Some heavily used areas have been stripped of dead wood for many yards in all directions.
- **Ease of cooking**: Cooking over an open fire is more difficult than on a stove.
- **Outside pan cleanup**: Pans blackened by wood fire cooking require more cleanup and more water.
- **Cleanliness**: Carbon black on the outside of pans will spread to almost everything in a pack, no matter how carefully packed.
- **Time required**: Cooking on an open fire requires more time: Gather the wood, light the fire, let it burn down, put the fire out, clean up the site and return it to a natural state.
- **Heat control**: The heat of fires cannot be regulated as well as that of a stove.
- **Smoke and odor**: I especially dislike the distraction of smoke in my eyes while I am preparing a meal and the burning wood smell permeates clothing and stays around for the rest of the trip.

People claim that using a stove that uses fossil fuels actually has more environmental impact than building a fire. They argue that using a stove only hides the impact by exporting it out of the wilderness. My response is that the objective of using a stove or similar technology is to minimize the impact of human presence in a particular location: the wilderness. Therefore, I am willing to export the impact and concentrate it in industrial production facilities that are as far from natural areas as possible.

The traditional open campfire keeps wildlife far away from camp and interferes with night vision so the beauty of the night is lost. Use a small candle lantern instead. A party grouped around this small flame is just as reassuring and comforting as being roasted and blinded by a large open fire. That warm, fuzzy campfire feeling comes from the social interaction of people in the group, not the physical presence of an open fire.

Pans

"The camp cook should take a pride in the artistic handling of his utensils, particularly in his ability to work quickly and to keep half a dozen things going at once…"
A. D. Gillette and S. McAndrew, *Outing* magazine, 1896

For many years, I used a far from ideal, but adequate (barely) three-piece aluminum MSR Alpine Cookset. The pans nested into a small easy-to-pack bundle, they stacked so multiple courses could be prepared on a single stove and it was lightweight and inexpensive. On the negative side, the pans didn't have a non-stick coating and cleaning was difficult. The aluminum was thin and didn't spread heat well so food tended to stick and the shiny aluminum didn't absorb heat as well as a dark surface.

Recently, I have been using a 7-piece non-stick pan set with 1, 1.5 and 2.5-liter pans with lids that double as fry pans. This is an almost perfect set of pans.

The number and sizes of pans allows the wilderness chef to select the right combination to take on a trip based on the number of people and menus.

The Ideal Set of Pans:

The ideal set of pans for lightweight cooking would:

- Be lightweight but heavy enough to spread heat evenly.
- Have a non-stick coating with rounded bottom corners.
- Stack one on top of the other.
- Have tight-fitting lids that can also be used as pans.
- Have lipped rims for strength.
- Nest together for storage.
- Have a dark finish to absorb heat readily.

Multiple-course meals using a one-burner stove

Multiple-course meals can be easily prepared using a set of pans that will stack and a single burner stove. Because a stack of two or three pans will have to be juggled, locate the kitchen area where there is a hard, level spot on which to set the stove that is far enough away from tents to discourage traffic in the area. Next, plan the order in which the courses of the meal will be prepared. Start with food that requires the largest pan and longest cooking time. While this course is cooking, prepare the next item on the menu in a smaller pan. When the first item is almost done, put the second item on the stove and use the first pan as the cover for the second (be sure the first pan has a lid too). Steam from the lower pan will heat the upper pan and continue cooking the food. Use a windscreen in cold or windy weather.

This procedure saves time and fuel and the various courses will be done at the same time and piping hot. I use this method with many dinner meals and occasionally juggle a stack of three pans.

Chef's tools and spice kit

To keep track of kitchen tools, I use a small folding zippered chef's kit available through most camping supply catalogs. The kit keeps the chef's tools clean and organized so I don't have to dig through the pockets of my pack to find everything needed to prepare a meal. The kit has pockets to organize chef's tools and elastic loop holders to hold small containers of spices.

The kit is also a safe haven for individual serving size condiments that I often carry that are available at fast food restaurants. The kit unzips and lies flat, providing a clean work surface that I can use to keep track of my cooking equipment. It also has a small loop that can be used to hang the kit from a handy limb. After a trip, the kit can be emptied and dropped into a washing machine to be ready for the next excursion.

In the kit, I carry a small sponge for cleanup, lexan cooking tools including a spoon and fork, rubber spatula for scraping food out of pots and a small set of measuring spoons. The contents of the small containers with spices and condiments change, depending on the particular menus planned for a trip. However, I always carry a small container of liquid anti-bacterial dish soap for cleanup, a bottle of vegetable oil, salt, pepper and sugar. Additional small containers for the kit are available from most outdoor camping suppliers.

Warning: *Do not* put spices in empty 35mm film canisters as some authors of outdoor books recommend.* Chemical residue from the film could possibly contaminate the spices and leave an odd taste. Film manufacturers have made public announcements stating not to use these containers for any sort of food storage. Buy new containers specifically made for food storage; they're cheap.

---

* A prominent supplier of outdoor equipment that sells devices through their catalog that clip on the top of a film canister to convert them to salt and pepper shakers. This is a bad idea, according to film manufacturers.

Food tubes

Imagine an oversized, translucent toothpaste tube with an open bottom that can be closed with a plastic clip. That's a food tube. To use a food tube, pack food into the tube through the open bottom, fold the bottom over and fasten it with the clip*. These indispensable food tubes can be used to carry peanut butter, margarine, honey, jelly, apple sauce, spaghetti and other sauces or just about anything that has a thick consistency. A food tube will hold anywhere from ½ to ¾ cups of food. To get the food out, remove the cap and squeeze like a tube of toothpaste*.

Don't scrimp and buy cheap tubes to save a dollar or two. A food tube blowout in a pack is not a pretty sight. To prevent leakage, carry them in a plastic bag and don't pack heavy or sharp-edged equipment on them. Better yet, carry them in an outside pocket for protection. The only disadvantage of using a food tube is how hard it is to clean after a trip. Soak the tubes in a pan of water for a couple of days before trying to remove the last of the food stuck to the inside.

Spices and condiments

"Spices wound our sense of taste; salt dresses the wound. Spices without salt make the mouth salivate after the feast is over…"

Malcolm de Chazal

"Condiments are like old friends—highly thought of, but often taken for granted."

Marilyn Kaytor, American writer

There is a long-held notion that anything cooked in the backcountry tastes great. False! Experience tells me that carrying a 40-pound pack or 75-pound

---

* Did you remember to put the cap on first?

* This, of course, starts the endless argument of which end of the tube to squeeze: bottom or top? I (rightly) squeeze it from the bottom.

canoe uphill in 90-plus degree temperatures for most of the day is probably the real source of this perception rather than actual taste of the food*.

The taste of a lot of camp food, especially dried food, can be bland and if the chef isn't careful, it all begins to taste the same. Adding small amounts of spices can improve the flavor dramatically. Digging through my spice cache at home, I discovered the following spices and condiments I have used in backcountry cooking at one time or other:

Spices:

- **Ground cinnamon:** used in baking and mixed with sugar for an unmistakable flavoring.
- **Sugar:** the all-purpose sweetener.
- **Garlic powder:** adds a little zip, but don't add too much of this strong flavor.
- **Onion powder:** adds a subtle pick-up to most meals.
- **Nutmeg:** used in baking muffins and spice breads.
- **Curry:** for that 'middle eastern' flavor.
- **Salt and pepper:** standard camp food spices; don't leave home without them.
- **Italian spice mix:** improves bland grocery store Italian meals.
- **Chili powder:** adds power to tomato-based meals and soups.
- **Cumin:** for that "south-of-the-border" flavor.
- **Maplene:** to flavor camp-made pancake syrup and baking.

---

* *The Law of Outdoor Meal Taste*: The Taste of a meal is equal to the Weight of the load, plus the absolute value of the maximum Slope of the trail, all multiplied by the number of Hours since the last meal. $T = (W + |S|) \times H$ For any calculation of T greater than 500, boiled rocks begin to taste good.

Condiments:

- **Ketchup and mustard**: standard American flavorings.
- **Mayonnaise**: put on sandwiches or for making your own salads.
- **Tartar sauce**: essential for the seafood lovers in the group.
- **Soy sauce**: for the taste of the Far East.
- **Non-dairy coffee creamer**: for small amounts of 'cream' and milk substitute.
- **Salsa**: a must for southwestern-flavored recipes.
- **Honey**: the world's finest sweetener.

Single-serving packages of the condiments above can be collected at fast food restaurants* or the deli section of supermarkets. The tear-off corners present a litter hazard, though.

- **Bouillon**: for chicken or beef flavorings.
- **Other dried soups**: use to pick up the flavor of most dinner meals.
- **Bacon bits**: add to eggs or sprinkle on top of stews, potatoes and soups.
- **Flavored breadcrumbs**: sprinkle on top of most meals for additional taste.
- **Salad topping mix**: shake onto most all rice and pasta meals.
- **Butter buds**: adds butter flavor to frying or baking.

To carry all of these on any one trip would require a separate backpack. So after reviewing the menu, I select spices and condiments to complement

---

* No, it's not necessary to actually eat at a fast food place to acquire single-serving packets of condiments (shudder!). Assign the task to junk food junkie friends who can handle such "cuisine."

the recipes and pack them in the chef's kit. Most recipes in this collection are not overly spiced and are palatable for most diners; but small quantities of spices can provide a boost for those who like a little more flavor.

Write the date on packages of spices and condiments. Over time, spices will lose their flavor and packaged condiments may spoil. Six to nine months is a normal shelf life for spices and three months for packages of condiments. Keep condiments in the refrigerator for long-term storage.

Outback Oven

Imagine preparing warm, freshly baked biscuits, bubbling sweet cherry cobbler with sugar glaze, dark chocolate brownies with walnuts, golden corn bread with syrup, thick crust pan pizza with pepperoni and other baked goods in the outdoors*.

Such goodies were traditionally only the providence of Dutch oven baking, but now there is a light-weight cooking accessory that makes baking in the wild not only possible, but easy: The Outback Oven.

In 1988, a Turkish bazaar provided parts for Rob and Diane Lerner to convert their single burner stove into a camp oven while they were on a 12,000-mile worldwide bicycle tour. When they returned to the United States, they refined the design and in the fall of 1991, the Outback Oven was born.

The Outback Oven consists of an aluminum pan with a non-stick coating and a domed lid with a thermometer attached as a lid knob. The pan sits on a ribbed aluminum heat diffuser plate placed over a stove burner. An aluminized fiberglass fabric convection dome goes over the whole thing to trap heat from the stove. The Oven comes with an aluminum collar that is attached under the burner of the stove to reflect heat upward from the stove into the convection dome and protect the attached fuel hose of the stove from overheating. The collar must be

---

* I just made myself hungry writing this sentence. Nothing adds more to a meal than fresh baked goodies.

trimmed with a knife or scissors to fit the particular stove that will be used with the Oven. All the parts fold neatly and fit inside of the pan, making a compact package that's easy to store and carry. I pack the parts in a heavy plastic bag to prevent scratching the non-stick surface of the pan.

When I first saw the Outback Oven I was extremely skeptical and didn't buy one for several years. It appeared to be bulky, complicated and had too many parts. First impressions were certainly wrong. The first weekend cooking with this ingenious device produced a tuna potpie, brownies and a pizza. I've been hooked on it ever since because almost anything that can be cooked in an oven at home can be made in camp using inexpensive foods found in any supermarket.

Once the contraption is set up, it's surprisingly easy to use. The food to be baked is mixed in the pan and covered. The pan is set on risers attached to a diffuser plate sitting on the stove burner and the fabric dome placed over everything. The Oven thermometer can be seen through an opening in the top of the dome. For the culinaryily challenged chef, the thermometer reads only "Warm-up", "Bake" and "Burn." Once the Oven is heated to the Bake range, all the cook has to do is adjust the stove flame to maintain the temperature at Bake and time the cooking.

There are a number of problems that can arise using the Outback Oven. A windscreen is essential. The Oven depends on the convection of heat upward from the stove so any significant wind will sharply increase cooking time. Also, the stove flame must be regulated carefully. If the flame is too high, the fiberglass dome can be scorched and the food will burn on the bottom; too low and the baking temperature will fall and the food will be undercooked. I use a stove such as the Peak 1 with the Oven because stoves such as the Whisperlight (notorious for its inability to maintain a low flame) require almost constant adjustments to maintain baking temperature.

On the other hand, all the fiddling and setup is worth the effort since once the temperature is in the Bake range, only a small flame is required to maintain baking temperatures. An estimated 1/3 less fuel is needed to prepare the meal compared with conventional cooking methods.

There are several models of the Outback Oven including the Ultralight, the Plus with an eight inch pan, the Plus 10 with a 10-inch pan and the Outfitter with a 12 inch pan. A variety of accessories are also available. There are several sources of prepackaged recipes for the Outback Oven, but I've never used them. They tend to be several times more expensive than conventional grocery store equivalents. Sources for these mixes are listed in Appendix III. All recipes in this collection were prepared in the Plus model with the 8 inch pan.

Not every stove can be used with the Outback Oven. The manufacturers of the Outback Oven include the following warning:

> **"Do not use Outback Oven with those Optimus, Svea or Primus stove models, or any stove that uses burner heat to pressurize fuel tank.**
>
> **Do not use Outback Oven with a windscreen that encloses fuel tank and stove together.**
>
> **Failure to follow these directions could result in a fuel tank explosion and serious injury."**

Therefore, be careful how the windscreen is set up and use a stove with a detached fuel tank such as the Peak 1 Apex or Whisperlight stove.

Many of the recipes in this collection use this cooking tool. Almost anything that can be prepared in a home oven can be quickly and easily made in this ingenious device.

Home Food Dryer:

"What was paradise but a garden full of vegetables [and] herbs…"
William Lawson

Mom was right; vegetables are good for you. They're an important part of a quality meal, providing taste, texture, flavor, color and significant nutrition. I like to have vegetables with every dinner either as part of a one-pot meal or as a side dish. Unfortunately, most commercial trail foods have few or no vegetables.

The problem is where to get a variety of dry vegetables inexpensively. There are many dried foods available, including rice, pasta, potatoes, fruits and some meat. Try to find dried vegetables at grocery stores, though! It's almost impossible to buy dried common garden vegetables such as green beans, corn, carrots and peas anywhere except at outdoor specialty stores or via a mail-order catalog. Commercially prepared dried garden vegetables are extremely expensive compared with their (undried) grocery store counterparts.

The solution is to prepare dried vegetables at home in a food dryer. The essential home food dryer is a stack of slotted plastic trays on which food is spread to dry and a base with a fan circulating warm air through the trays, all covered with a clear dome lid. Food dryers cost anywhere from about $30 to more than $100. The difference in cost between inexpensive grocery store vegetables dried at home and expensive commercially prepared vegetables will quickly pay the price of a home food dryer.

A dryer comes with a detailed book of instructions on how to dry raw foods and there are a number of books available that explain the process. However, I rarely dry raw foods. Instead, for trail use, I dry canned vegetables. Dehydrating fresh raw vegetables works well, but after being reconstituted, they still must be cooked which takes more time and fuel. Canned vegetables, on the other hand, have been cooked as part of the canning process and are ready to eat after being reconstituted. I have dried peas, carrots, green and yellow beans, corn, Chinese vegetables, sweet potatoes, pearl onions, mushrooms, black beans and beets (once!).

Drying canned vegetables is easy. Here are the steps:

- **Clean workspace and tools:** Wash all your tools, your hands, drying trays and counter surfaces with hot soapy water. Rinse everything in hot water.

- **Select quality brands of vegetables:** Generic or off-brand vegetables are not as flavorful and the vegetable pieces are not as uniform in size, which can cause uneven drying.

- **Choose vegetables cut into the smallest pieces possible:** Instead of whole green beans select 'French cut' and 'Julienne sliced' carrots since they will dry faster and more evenly. They also reconstitute faster.

- **Choose 'low' or 'reduced' sodium brands:** Some canned vegetables have so much added salt that it overwhelms the flavor of the vegetables.

- **Pour the vegetables into a colander and rinse well:** This helps separate the vegetable pieces so they can be spread easily on the trays and it further reduces the salt.

- **Recycle the empty cans:** Peel the labels and recycle the paper and the can.

- **Spread the vegetables evenly on the drying racks:** Each rack in my dryer holds the contents of one 14 to16-ounce can of vegetables. Avoid clumps of vegetable pieces since this will cause uneven drying.

- **Dry for 5 to 8 hours:** How long to dry vegetables will depend on how soon they will be used. For a weekend trip, dry them for about 5 hours or until they have a leathery and pliable texture. For longer trips or if they will be in storage, dry them for about 8 hours or until they are hard and brittle.

- **Don't interrupt the drying process:** Mold and bacteria will grow on partially dried vegetables. If the drying process is interrupted, these microorganisms can begin to grow.

- **Packing and storage:** Pack the dried vegetables into a locking plastic bag and force out as much air as possible. Store in the refrigerator until needed for a trip.

- **Dry just before use:** Dry vegetables only a few days before they will be used.
- **Refrigerate:** Refrigerate dried vegetables that have been packed until they are actually taken on the trail to retard growth of microorganisms.

The difference in cost between inexpensive grocery store vegetables dried at home and expensive commercially prepared vegetables will quickly pay the cost of a home food dryer. A two-serving package of commercial freeze-dried vegetables will cost from $2.50 to $3.75 as of the time of this writing. The same canned vegetables dried at home will cost from 45 to 60 cents plus a little labor. I can dry 5 cans of vegetables at a time in my dryer, so I save $10 to $15 on each batch of vegetables compared to the cost of commercial freeze-dried vegetables.

Home-drying vegetables not only saves money, but it reduces their weight significantly. The following table illustrates the difference in weight of vegetables directly from the can and after drying.

Canned Vegetable	Beginning Weight (Drained)	Dry Weight
Green beans	7 ounces	¾ ounce
Whole corn	9½ ounces	3 ounces
Peas (small)	9 ounces	2 ounces
Carrots (diced)	9½ ounces	1 ounce

I also dry tomato paste, salsa and spaghetti sauce. The food dryer has plastic overlays that cover the slots in each tray so that sauces can be spread over a large surface area. When most of the liquid is evaporated in about 6 to 8 hours, a sauce will have the texture of fruit leather or a fruit rollup and can be rolled from the tray with a plastic spatula and stored in a plastic bag.

Dried foods should be refrigerated in sealed plastic bags if they won't be used right away. Dry vegetables only a few days before the trip on which they will be eaten. For food safety, treat all food that is rehydrated as if it was fresh and always bring it to a boil even momentarily to be sure harmful microorganisms have been destroyed.

-Two-

Camp Health and Sanitation

Safe food handling

Recent outbreaks of disease caused by *E. coli* and salmonella bacteria contaminating improperly cooked or prepared food are stark warnings that safe food is essential to everyone's health. This is particularly true in relatively primitive camp meal preparation.

Contaminated food is much more common than most people know. A recent study conducted by the Centers for Disease Control indicated the surprising statistics that 76 million Americans suffer from some form of food poisoning annually and almost 5,000 die as a result. In spite of extensive media coverage of food-borne illnesses, surveys document a number of misconceptions that prevent people from changing risky food handling habits:

- Many people believe foodborne illness is just a relatively mild gastrointestinal distress that occurs shortly after eating when, in fact, it can be fatal and symptoms may not appear for a day or more.

- Most people are only aware of food safety problems they can see or smell, such as spoilage. Food may not appear spoiled, but can still be contaminated with microorganisms. *It is not possible to tell if food is contaminated by appearance or odor alone.*

- To many Americans, used to an extremely safe food supply, foodborne illness is a remote issue—something that happens to other people in other countries. It can happen to anyone if precautions aren't taken.

To promote food safety, the Partnership for Food Safety Education was formed in 1996 to combine resources of the federal government, food industry and consumer groups*. The organization recommends that anyone working with food in any capacity practice these four key techniques to keep bacteria away from food:

- **Clean:** Wash hands, utensils and surfaces with hot soapy water before and after food preparation. Especially after preparing meat, poultry, eggs or seafood.

- **Separate:** Don't cross-contaminate foods. Cross-contamination of foods occurs when uncooked foods in which bacteria grow rapidly come into contact with already prepared foods. This generally happens with raw meats, dairy products and fresh-caught fish

- **Thorough cooking:** Cook foods to proper temperatures. Cooking foods to boiling temperatures while preparing a meal will kill dangerous microorganisms. Never eat foods not brought to a boil or meats cooked rare.

- **Chill:** Keep raw and perishable foods cold before preparation. Refrigerate foods at a temperature of 40 degrees F or less within 2 hours of cooking.

These four techniques to fight bacteria are excellent general guidelines for food safety, however they apply primarily to home food preparation. Safe food handling and preparation in camp without refrigeration or large quantities of hot water present significantly more challenges to the wilderness chef. Food safety is a continuous process that must be integrated into all parts of outdoor meal preparation: planning meals, selecting food,

---

* The Partnership for Food Safety Education can be reached at www.fightbac.org on the web.

preparation in camp and cleanup after a meal. The following guidelines for safe food handling and preparation are recommended:

Food selection:

- **Types of foods**: Choose dried, canned or processed foods, especially meats, instead of raw. The recipes in this collection use canned, processed, or dried meats or no meat at all.

- **Raw foods**: If raw foods are chosen for meals, work out a method to keep them cold and plan menus in such a way to use those foods on the first days of a trip.

- **Packaging**: Don't damage the packaging of foods. Damaged packaging allows bacteria in and leakage may contaminate other foods.

- **Portion size**: Plan menus and prepare foods for groups of two to four people. Small quantities of food can be brought to a boil faster and leftovers are minimized. The majority of menus listed in this collection are designed for two to four people.

Food Preparation:

- **Clean hands**: The chef should always wash his or her hands before preparing meals. Follow the directions for an effective, bacteria killing method using only small amounts of water.

  Hot water is a limited wilderness commodity and large quantities are simply not available for traditional hand washing. The following backcountry technique, using a minimum of hot water can be used to get clean hands:

  1. Wet hands thoroughly with treated water.

  2. Add a small amount of germicidal soap.

  3. Work up lather by scrubbing hands together, especially around fingernails.

4. Clean under fingernails.

5. Rinse thoroughly with treated water.

6. Repeat soap lather and rinse.

7. Dry with a clean towel or bandana or air dry.

Tests have shown this technique provides adequate hand sanitation using only about a half liter of clean water. Always use clean, treated or boiled water and move at least 200 feet away from any sources of water before using soap.

- **Utensils:** Use clean utensils and prepare food on clean surfaces. Most recipes can be prepared directly in clean pans. Storing utensils in a clean pouch or bag that can be closed is essential to keep your chef's tools clean.

- **Meats:** Cook meats thoroughly. Never eat meats, especially hamburger, that are not cooked thoroughly (no pink left).

- **Clean water:** Use only treated water for cooking.

- **Bacteria in foods:** Boiling will kill bacteria. Bring all foods to a boil even for a short time.

- **Cross-contamination:** Keep untreated water away from the food preparation area to avoid contaminating clean cooking utensils and surfaces.

- **Reconstituted food:** Handle dried food that has been rehydrated exactly as if it was fresh.

- **Cooked food:** Once any food, even dried food, is rehydrated or cooked it must be eaten, stored properly or discarded.

- **Chilling:** Cooked food must be chilled to 40 degrees F or less within 2 hours of preparation.

- **Final cleanup:** Clean all cooking equipment thoroughly with germicidal dish soap and treated water.

Personal and common equipment:

- **Personal utensils**: Don't allow personal utensils in community pans—use separate serving spoons.
- **Water bottles**: Don't share water bottles with other members of the party.
- **GORP**: Provide individual packages of snacks and trail mix.
- **Cleanliness**: Insist that all individual equipment be cleaned after every meal.
- **Clean water**: Be sure that each person in the group has adequate water treatment equipment.
- **Illness**: Any person showing symptoms of illness should be prevented from handling food or preparing meals.

Any illness caused by contaminated food is serious in the backcountry where medical help may be hours or days away. Safe food handling procedures are simple and require only small changes in habits and awareness. They may save a life—perhaps yours.

Safe water supply

A high mountain lake with cold clear water or a sparkling stream rushing down a hillside in a remote wilderness area would seem to be safe to drink. Not anymore! Studies have found pathogens in a large percentage of the world's water supply. Since harmful organisms are microscopic in size, it's impossible to determine if a water supply is contaminated by appearance alone. As a general rule, treat all water unless it comes from a known treated supply.

There are many ways of treating water including boiling, chemical treatments such as iodine, bleach and halazone products and filtering*. From a cook's point of view, boiling is slow and requires a lot of fuel. Chemical treatments leave an objectionable chemical taste in even highly spiced food. Use a water filter for all cooking and drinking water to avoid both problems; it requires no fuel and leaves no taste.

Establishing a safe water supply in the wilderness with the least impact requires thought, planning and technique. Here are some guidelines:

- **Camp arrangement**: Set up camp a minimum of 200 feet from any water supply.

- **Large water containers**: Carry a large collapsible water container to be used in camp to minimize the number of trips made to the water supply. Only a few trips will create an obvious trail.

- **Transfer of water**: Pour water from the larger container into smaller containers for treatment.

- **Cross Contamination**: Don't pour untreated water into clean cooking equipment or mix untreated with treated water.

- **Boiling water**: To kill microorganisms, bring all food to boiling even if for only a short time.

- **Cleanup**: Use clean treated water for all camp cleanup chores.

- **Distance from water sources**: Never wash dishes or carry out any personal hygiene activities in or near any body of water.

Protecting food from animals

Improper food storage is the wilderness equivalent of posting an open house sign in front of camp inviting animals in for a midnight snack. The

---

* A more detailed discussion of the pros and cons of various water treatment methods can be found in the books in Appendix III.

lure of food will attract all sorts of unwanted visitors including small (rodents), medium (raccoons, porcupines), large (coyotes, deer) and extra large (bears, moose) sizes of prowlers.

Preventing animal incursions begins with the physical arrangement of camp.

- **Camp arrangement**: Set up camp in the shape of a large triangle with sides approximately 100 yards long. At one apex, set up the food preparation area; at another the sleeping area; and at the third, food storage.

- **Food preparation area**: Do all cooking and eating in the food preparation area.

- **Cook carefully**: Dispose of trash and don't not spill any food particles that will attract animals.

- **Sleeping area**: Never keep any food in the sleeping area—this is last place in camp where midnight visitors would be welcome.

- **Food storage**: Store all food and other equipment in the food storage area. I routinely hoist my pack off the ground with rope over a tree limb to keep animals away from my equipment. Small animals will chew pads and belts for the salt and gnaw holes in pockets.

- **Bear country**: Put the food storage area as much as 200 yards from the sleeping area and go to the extra effort of bear bagging food and other smellable items. (Bear bagging is explained in detail in a number of references in Appendix III).

Disposal of packaging, leftovers and wastewater

Preparing, eating and cleaning up after a meal always produces leftover food, packaging and wastewater. Proper handling of these is an on-going process beginning at home before the trip and ending at home after the trip.

Home preparation:

- Repackage food to minimize packaging that will have to be carried.
- Plan meal portions carefully so there will be few, if any, leftovers.
- Avoid greasy meat-based meals, which are harder to clean up. The odor of empty packages that contained meat will attract animals.
- Bring several extra locking plastic bags in which to carry waste food for disposal later.
- Purchase a pan set with non-stick surfaces so leftover food can be easily removed from the sides and bottoms of the pans.

Choosing the kitchen location:

- Find a spot at least 200 feet from any water source and 200 feet from the camp area.
- Locate the kitchen on a trample-resistant surface that will not be damaged from the traffic in the kitchen.
- Use an existing campsite, if there is one, rather than making a new site.
- Concentrate all food activities, preparation, dining and cleanup in one spot to prevent spreading food particles over a wide area.

Handling food and packaging:

- Cook and clean up at the same time. Have a locking plastic bag next to the food preparation area into which all packaging will go.
- Carefully mix ingredients and avoid spilling any particles of food. These food particles, small as they are, will attract animals.
- Pick up food particles after each meal so they are not ground into the soil. Put food particles into the food waste bag.

- Don't let foods boil over, making cleanup more difficult and causing food particles to fall to the ground.

Doing the dishes:

- Establish a cleanup area away from the camping, cooking and food storage areas and at least 200 feet from any water source.
- Dig a sump to strain the wastewater into what is leftover from cleanup. To dig a sump, carefully clear an area about 1 foot in diameter, setting aside the organic material on top of the soil. Dig about 6 to 8 inches deep, piling up the soil next to the hole.
- *Never* clean or rinse dishes in or near any body of water.
- Do dishes immediately after a meal. The longer they sit, the more food particles will stick to pans, even non-stick pans.
- Carry a small rubber spatula to scrape clean pans and other dishes.
- After scraping, put all leftover food into a locking plastic food waste bag that will be carried out. Don't mix food with the bag that has leftover packaging.
- Wash pans with hot water and a scrubbing sponge without soap. Soap is unnecessary if the menu does not include greasy meat-based foods.
- If soap is required, use a tiny drop (so small it can just be seen) of concentrated germicidal detergent per pan.
- When the pan is clean, pour the leftover water through a strainer to remove any food particles into the sump. The water can be strained though a small wire strainer, a piece of coffee filter, bandana, or even fingers.
- Pack the strained scraps into the food waste bag to reduce odors and pack them out.

- Carefully fill in the sump and return the area to a natural state by spreading ground cover over the site of the sump.

Site cleanup:

- Examine the area used for food preparation and pick up food particles and scraps of packaging; even the tiniest piece. If it can seen, pick it up!
- Return the site to a natural appearance.

Post-trip:

- Properly dispose of waste foods and packaging by recycling or reusing.
- Determine what meals had leftovers and either change the quantities of the recipe ingredients to reduce the excess or use a different recipe.
- For safety reasons, discard any open packages of unused food. Save food that is still sealed for another meal.
- Go through the packaging carried out to determine if there are ways of reducing the amount carried in.
- Clean the plastic bags used to carry meals and reuse. Heavy duty plastic bags can safely be put in boiling water.

Cooking safely in the wilderness with the least environmental impact is significantly more difficult than at home. Taking time to plan the process of meal preparation and cleanup and acquiring some new habits will allow the chef to produce quality meals and protect the health of the party.

-Three-

The Food

"I always eat from the four food groups every day; breakfast, lunch, dinner and snacks."

Garfield the cat

It amazes me that some people will buy expensive hardware such as packs and sleeping bags and then scrimp on the quality of food for the essential software; their bodies. Good food is far more than just a source of fuel for outdoor adventures. A well-prepared meal provides sufficient calories and nutrition for vigorous outdoor activities. It's also a morale booster and three times per day social event.

Outdoor food falls into two categories: commercially prepared meals and meals made from ingredients that can be purchased at any hometown grocery store.

Commercially Prepared Foods

"…backpacking is a refined sport, noted for lightness…. [Backpackers] carry two little packets from which they can spread out a nine-course meal. One packet contains the food and the other a freeze-dried French chef."

Patrick F. McManus

A French chef (even a freeze-dried one), faced with the challenge of preparing satisfying meals for a week using only commercially prepared outdoor foods, would probably cook his hat in despair. I was on a week-long trip where all food, provided by an outfitter, was the freeze-dried outdoor meal type. A meal was "cooked"* by pouring boiling water into a bag, stirring and waiting 5 minutes. The resulting meal was an oddly colored amorphous glop of indeterminate taste with a texture like that of thick wallpaper paste with lumps. It was a mechanical process, aesthetically unsatisfactory and lacked the pleasure of spending time to prepare and consume a meal with friends.

To add injury to insult, the amount of food per person in a four-portion dinner was so ridiculously small, the trip turned into a contest of who would lose the most weight. These meals were morale busters. They were dreaded but it was eat them or starve.

I have three concerns about commercially prepared dehydrated or freeze-dried foods: cost, serving size and taste.

- **Cost per serving per meal**: A full dinner meal can cost as much $6 per person. Purchasing food at a grocery store will reduce the cost by 50 percent or more. On longer trips of a week or more, this will make a huge difference; with a large group there will be a savings of hundreds of dollars.

- **Serving size**: The volume of food and number of calories provided by commercial freeze-dried foods is not large enough by at least half. Four-man serving packets were enough for only two. Outdoor activities require large numbers of calories and sufficient volume of food to fill the empty corners of an appetite.

- **Taste**: Taste, texture and flavor are the hallmarks of a satisfying quality meal. With commercial foods, all three are sacrificed for ease of preparation. Each meal looks like every other meal and after a few

---

* This method of cooking should be offensive to anyone claiming to be a wilderness chef. It's like having Thanksgiving dinner at a fast food joint.

days menu doldrums set in. Every meal should be an event that everyone looks forward to. Adequate nutrition and calories are essential for outdoor activities. Well-prepared meals with a variety of flavors and textures that are tempting in appearance will encourage trail-weary travelers to consume sufficient quantities of food to fuel heavy outdoor activities.

Grocery Store Foods

"Among us we had dried beef, fried ham, cold boiled eggs, sardines, bread and butter, extract of beef, cheese, chocolate, dried peaches, raisins and prunes."

Fay Fuller; first woman to climb Mt. Rainier, 1890

Appalachian Trail Hiker's Food Choices:

If commercially prepared trail food has so many drawbacks, what foods do people eat in the wilderness? Consider the menus of Appalachian Trail (AT) through-hikers. They spend months on the trail where they plan, carry and prepare hundreds of meals. What kinds of foods do they carry? A survey of AT through-hikers found that almost all avoid specially packaged, dehydrated or freeze-dried foods because of the small portions and high cost. Instead, they planned their meals around common supermarket foods. Listed below are the most common foods reported by AT hikers in the survey:

Breakfasts:
Cold cereal with powdered milk
Instant oatmeal
Toaster pastries
Eggs (fresh and dry)

Bread with peanut butter
Bagels with peanut butter or cream cheese
Candy bars
Granola bars
GORP with powdered milk
Pancakes
Granola in powdered milk
Instant potatoes such as hash browns

Lunches:

Sardines
Cheese
Nuts
Crackers (graham or variety)
Beef jerky, pepperoni, or other dried meats
Peanut butter and jelly sandwiches
Dried soups
Candy bars
English muffins, bagels or other breads and peanut butter
Corned beef or Spam®
Tuna
Dried fruits
Granola bars
Snack foods
GORP (a mixture of nuts, raisins, M&Ms®, sunflower seeds, dried
cereal, etc.)

Dinners:

Flavored instant rice

Macaroni and cheese (staple food often with meat, tuna, or dried soup added)
Flavored noodle dinners
Instant stuffing
Instant soup
Ramen noodles
Pasta salads
Flavored instant potato dinners
Instant gravies and cheese sauces added to potato, rice, noodle and stuffing mixes
Tuna and other canned or dried meats used with any mixes listed above

Beverages

Water
Powdered fruit drinks already sweetened
Powdered ice tea, fruit teas, or flavored tea
Flavored gelatin mix as a hot drink
Hot tea
Cocoa/hot chocolate
Instant coffee

Desserts

Instant puddings with powdered milk
Instant cheesecake
Cookies
Flavored gelatin
Dried fruits

The Never-ending Quest for Perfect Wilderness Foods

"Supermarkets are as conspiratorial as any Las Vegas casino. All along those innocent-looking aisles, to the backdrop of piped-in bouncy showtunes, are alimentary ambushes."

Bryan Miller, *New York Times* restaurant critic

One of the wilderness chef's small joys in life is to explore a large grocery store for the first time, especially one in or near a major city. Poking around in the ethnic food sections and peering among the shelves in long aisles of familiar foods in search of a new or unusual product that can be used to create a different camp meal is close to culinary nirvana.

Like the search for the fountain of youth, the quest for perfect wilderness foods is never ending. Such delights are just around the corner in the next aisle. Just keep looking.

Characteristics of perfect wilderness foods:

- **Low cost:** Meals should not cost significantly more than home-prepared meals.
- **Substantial serving size:** There should be enough to feed someone who has been exercising strenuously for hours at a time.
- **Variable serving size:** The chef should be able to vary the amount of food prepared in a given recipe to accommodate different numbers of campers and different sized appetites. Commercially prepared food comes in a one-size-fits-all serving size.
- **Easy to prepare:** Preparation of a meal should be simple and relatively foolproof.

- **Preparation time**: Time needed to prepare a meal should be a short as possible.
- **Variety**: Large variety prevents meal-boredom.
- **Nutritious**: Each meal should provide sufficient nutrients for someone engaged in hard outdoor recreation.
- **Lightweight**: Don't carry any more weight than necessary.
- **Dry**: Water can be added later and not carried. Dry food will not spoil.
- **Compact**: Small volume that does not fill up a pack.
- **Non-perishable**: Eliminates spoilage and keeps food safe even in the summer.
- **Little packaging**: Avoid buying foods packaged in metal or glass containers. Buy foods that can be repacked into smaller, lighter containers.
- **Good appearance and texture**: Commercial trail food tends to look and taste the same after a few days. Quality camp food should look and taste like real food.
- **High calorie density**: Carry foods that provide lots of calories per weight and volume.

Grocery stores have a lot of almost perfect foods, including dried fruits, rice, pasta and rice dinners, breakfast bars, flavored potato mixes, baking mixes, dried meats, peanut butter, dried soups, stuffing mixes, sauces and breads. Using these as a base for meal planning, it's possible to create many recipes that are almost perfect trail meals.

There is one food, usually not available in grocery stores, that is a perfect trail food and is used in many recipes. It's a meat substitute called Textured Vegetable Protein or (TVP) for short.

Textured Vegetable Protein (TVP) as a meat substitute

Preparing meals containing meat on a trip of more than a few days presents a number of significant problems. Fresh meat is heavy and will not last more than a day or so before it spoils. Canned and dried meats are expensive, heavy and come in packaging that must be carried out. Also, the odor of empty containers will attract animals for the rest of the trip. There is an alternative to fresh meat; textured vegetable protein (TVP).

I'll admit TVP looks like dry dog food*; certainly not something suitable for human consumption no matter how hungry or far out in the wilderness you find yourself. First impressions, however, are misleading. Those dry chunks are a healthy, all-natural meat substitute made from soybeans.

TVP is created by combining soybeans, which are almost 40 percent protein, with wheat gluten to create flour. The oil is extracted and the flour pressure-cooked so the protein and gluten bond. It's then shaped, textured, dried and sometimes flavored.

Most people may have never heard of TVP, but food producers have been using this meat-substitute for more than 25 years in a variety of prepared products. Generally it can be found in the ingredients list on the package under the alias of "hydrolyzed vegetable protein" or "textured soy flour."

The nutritional credentials of TVP are impressive: It's all-natural; has almost no fat or cholesterol; is high in protein, potassium, calcium and magnesium; low in calories and contains all eight essential amino acids. For trail meals it's the perfect food. It's dry, light in weight and can't spoil. It's easy to use and inexpensive; a one pound package of unflavored TVP costs less than $3 and is the equivalent of 6 pounds of meat.

---

* While working with a Boy Scout Troop teaching Scouts how to use TVP for their campout meals, I saw the boys had listed TVP on a dinner menu as "Gravy Train."

TVP comes in a variety of textures and colorings and can be purchased in health food stores and by mail. There are caramel-colored granules to substitute for hamburger, chunks that can be used in stews and larger slices called strip steak. There are similar light-colored textures for chicken substitutes.

Although some TVP is flavored, I prefer it plain so it can be flavored according to demands of the recipe. Generally, an equivalent amount of TVP can be substituted for meat in a recipe. Once reconstituted, a new dimension in cooking for the wilderness chef opens. It can be made into meatballs, burgers and put into stews, soups and sauces. I have used TVP to make pizza toppings, fajitas, stir-fry, tacos, spaghetti, stews, barbecue, chili and other meals that require meat. TVP can be flavored with beef or chicken bouillon, packaged spices, dried soup, or gravy mixes found at any grocery store.

Flavored TVP includes barbecue, taco, pork, bacon, sausage and pepperoni. I have tried a number of different varieties of flavored TVP and prefer plain since it provides more flexibility in creating meals. Flavored TVP is also more than twice as expensive as unflavored and contains much more salt, MSG and fat compared to unflavored.

TVP is reconstituted by mixing with an equal amount of water. One pound of cooked meat is the equivalent of ¾ cup of TVP combined with ¾ cup of water. In any recipe that uses TVP, I always use one cup each of TVP and water since it's easier and more accurate to measure in a camp cup.

To use as a meat substitute in recipes, mix the TVP, flavoring (bouillon, dry soup or gravy mixes) and water as the first step to prepare a meal. Then prepare the recipe as if it contained meat. To decrease cooking time, put the TVP and water in a pan to reconstitute as soon as camp is set up.

Many recipes use TVP, but fresh, canned, or dried meats can be used instead. To use meats, eliminate the TVP, one cup of water used to reconstitute the TVP and the flavoring.

Textured vegetable protein is usually not available in grocery stores. It can be found in some health food stores, but it's overpriced and there is little variety. It's available via mail and well worth the time to order some and try it. Sources for buying TVP are listed in Appendix III.

Packing and Organizing Meals

"Having problems finding your toothpicks in your pack?…Did you find a cereal bar that had been at the bottom of your pack since Richard Nixon was president and eat it anyway?"

Chris Kallio

Like the real estate agent's mantra of "location, location, location," the key to successful meal preparation is "organization, organization, organization." There is nothing more frustrating than conducting a pack-to-pack search before a meal can be prepared. Organizing meals at home vastly simplifies meal preparation on the trail.

Grocery store food packaging:

Foods in grocery stores are over-packaged. In some cases, packaging actually weighs and costs more than the food. On average, 20 percent of the weight of groceries is packaging and 10 percent of the price is required to pay for it. This doesn't include the bags used at the checkout (paper or plastic?) where there seems to be a contest to see how many bags can be used for one order.

There are many ways to reduce the packaging of foods purchased at the store and what has to be taken on the trail.

Waste-watchers tips (reduce-reuse-recycle):

At the store:

- **Buy in bulk:** Bulk purchases save money and reduce packaging. Some food cooperatives allow customers to bring their own containers.
- **Buy the largest containers available:** There is less packaging per unit of food in larger containers. This is a good strategy only if food isn't wasted because the container is too big.

- **Buy foods in recyclable containers**: Purchase food in containers that can be recycled through community recycling programs.
- **Prewrapped produce**: Don't buy produce in shrink-wrapped packages. Buy loose produce and reuse the plastic bags provided by the store. When the bag is no longer usable, recycle it.
- **Recycle plastic bags**: Many grocery stores now have places to drop off used bags for recycling.
- **Buy reusable tote bags**: Take your own reusable canvas bags (with handles) to pack your groceries in at the checkout*.
- **Small plastic bags**: When buying locking plastic bags to organize menu items for a trip, choose rugged freezer bags. They can be washed out and reused.

Repackaging food at home:

- **Food tubes**: Use reusable food tubes for peanut butter, honey, jelly, thick sauces, etc.
- **Small food containers**: Small plastic bottles for spices and other small food items are available from camping supply catalogs.
- **Recycle**: Recycle as much packaging as possible.
- **Reuse**: Reuse plastic bags from previous trips.
- **Other sources of bags**: Save and reuse bread wrappers and other plastic bags from the grocery store to pack food. Recycle when they get ragged.

---

* Nothing confuses a grocery store checkout bagger more than when I respond to the "paper or plastic" question with "neither." It gets some odd looks from other customers in line, too.

On the trail:

- **Pack it in, pack it out**: If it can be carried in full, it can be carried out empty.
- **Waste disposal**: Don't burn anything; don't bury anything.
- **Open packages carefully**: Don't drop small tear-off pieces of packages.
- **Cook and clean up at the same time**: Don't let debris accumulate; it's easy to lose small bits of trash.
- **Use a trash bag**: Pack empty food containers inside of another locking plastic bag to consolidate trash and reduce odors.
- **Be a neat cook**: Don't drop food particles around the cooking area.
- **Pick up after others**: Pick up trash and litter others have left and pack it out.

Back home:

- **Recycle:** Sort through the trash hauled out and recycle as much as possible.
- **Reuse:** Clean plastic bags and reuse them if possible.
- **Plan for the next trip:** After looking through the refuse carried out, determine if there is anything that could have been eliminated by organizing or packing food differently.

Repackaging food:

Everyone who travels in the backcountry should give a special award to the person who invented the locking plastic bag. Locking plastic bags in a variety of sizes from snack to gallon are indispensable and I use them extensively for repackaging foods and as meal organizers.

The objectives of repackaging are to:

- Reduce the packaging weight and volume that will have to be carried on the trip and then back out again.
- Recycle excess packaging.
- Premix dry ingredients to reduce time and effort to prepare a recipe.
- Organize food into meal groups.

To repackage a meal, collect all ingredients for that particular meal and examine the packaging. Determine which containers can be eliminated (especially boxes) and transfer the contents into locking plastic bags. At the same time, measure and mix dry ingredients according to instructions. Each recipe in this collection has a section titled "Home Preparation" to help guide this process.

Organizing:

Meal organization is a way to keep all ingredients for a particular recipe in one place so they can be found easily at mealtimes and divide up the weight of food so that it can be fairly distributed between members of the party. There are several ways of organizing meals depending on length of trip, number in the party and personal preference.

- **Whole day:** Put all meals for a particular day in a single bag.
- **One meal at a time:** Pack each complete meal in a separate bag.
- **All meals together:** Put all the breakfasts in one bag, lunches in another, etc.
- **Bulk bagging:** In one bag, put all the coffee, drinks, instant oatmeal, etc.

My preference is to pack food one meal to a bag. Take each item required by the recipe and discard any excess packaging. Repackage as needed and put all items for that particular meal in a one-gallon size plastic bag. Write the name of the meal such as Friday dinner, Sunday breakfast, etc. on the outside of the bag with a permanent-marking pen. If there are instructions printed on a package, write them on the outside of the bag or cut the instructions from the package and drop them in the bag. I usually have a few bulk bags containing such things as drinks, bags of trail snacks and instant oatmeal.

-Four-

The Recipes

"A…meal is a story told from nature, taking its rhythms, its humors, its bounty and turning them into episodes for the senses."
Marcella Hazan, Italian cookbook author

"Eating is not merely a material pleasure. Eating well gives a spectacular joy to life and contributes immensely to good will and happy companionship. It is of great importance to the morale."
Elsa Schiaparelli

Finally: the recipes. For those who have jumped directly to the recipes[*] and skipped everything else, I reiterate a point made in the introduction. This is a collection of favorite recipes using equipment like the Outback Oven and foods such as TVP and home-dried vegetables which may not be familiar to some readers. I recommend that before getting too far into the recipes that you read the sections describing this equipment and food to better understand the recipes and how they are prepared.

The general strategy to prepare a recipe is that almost all of the measuring and mixing is done at home. There may be as many as three separate plastic bags for a recipe, but they are combined in the order given. In camp, all the chef has to do is mix water and the ingredients in the correct order and cook.

---

[*] I'll confess. I do this too. I want to get to the meat of the book right away just like you do.

43

There are a few general guidelines that I have learned from experience about preparing these recipes:

- **Time:** Contrary to a popular saying, food in a watched pot will indeed boil and then promptly burn. Watch the time carefully and don't leave any meal unattended while it's cooking, even for the briefest time[*].

- **Water:** The amount of water listed in the "Ingredients" section is *not* an exact measure. The exact amount of water needed depends on brand of food and size of the package, which varies. So, unless the recipe is made exactly with the same brands, sizes and combinations of food I used, (extremely unlikely) the recipe will probably require slightly more or less water. It's a good practice to have about ½ cup of water handy to add as needed. There are two rules about adding water to a recipe:

   Rule one: Always add a little at a time; a tablespoon or less.
   Rule two: Water can always added, but it can't be taken out.

- **Fresh or canned meats:** I am not vegetarian, but many of the recipes use TVP (textured vegetable protein, see Chapter III) instead of fresh or canned meats. Fresh or canned meats can be substituted for the TVP. Almost all recipes, except for breakfast, use the equivalent of approximately ¾ pound of fresh or canned meat. Sources where TVP can be purchased by mail are listed in Appendix III. I have often prepared meals using TVP instead of meat for unsuspecting diners who didn't realize it was not meat.

- **Leftovers:** Although dry ingredients will not spoil under normal outdoor conditions, as soon as ingredients are reconstituted spoilage can begin. Therefore, *as soon as water has been added, all foods must be handled and treated as if they were fresh.* Prepare meals immediately, keep

---

[*] In fact, the speed at which food will boil over or burn is equal to the cube of the time the pot is not watched.

foods cool if possible and either eat or properly dispose of leftovers. *Unless there is a way of keeping them cool, do not carry and eat leftovers from a previous meal.* Plan meals so that there will be few, if any, leftovers.

All recipes can be prepared on a single burner stove. Some recipes require several courses, which can be prepared on additional stoves or a multi-burner stove, but it isn't necessary. Using one stove reduces the weight of the kitchen by eliminating equipment and fuel. (A description of cooking multiple courses on a single burner stove is in Chapter II.) Previous juggling experience, although helpful, is not required.

Finally, enjoy preparing these recipes. If you don't like to cook, find someone in the party who does and swap cleanup chores with him or her. A wilderness chef who enjoys preparing good meals makes any trip vastly better for everyone. The wilderness chef should always remember:

"One laughs when joyous, sulks when angry and is at peace with the world when the stomach is satisfied."

Hawaiian Proverb

Beverages:

I confess. I'll admit it. I hate coffee, despise tea and refuse to drink any and all of their variations*. As a result, I am often out of step with my companions who carry a lot of coffee and tea making equipment to brew the stuff at every opportunity. I have tried to make coffee and have had my efforts so enthusiastically criticized that I have given up any future attempts. There are many other beverage choices that I like, including my favorite recipe for hot chocolate.

---

* Why anyone would pay three bucks or more for one cup of fancy coffee is beyond me!

No matter what your personal preference for beverages is, remaining adequately hydrated is important—to the point of survival. People can survive a surprisingly long time without food; many days in fact. Without water, depending on the temperature and climate, someone may be in danger after only a few hours. Water is also essential for peak physical performance. As soon as the body starts to run a water deficit, the ability to do strenuous outdoor activities declines precipitously.

How much water is necessary varies from person to person depending on weather conditions and activity level. Warnings of incipient dehydration include a reduction in urine output and change in its color. Dark urine indicates a water deficit; the lighter, the better.

Ideally, wilderness travelers should attempt to remain hydrated at all times. Preventing dehydration is an ongoing process beginning at breakfast and continuing throughout the day.

Some suggestions for remaining hydrated through the day are:

- **Morning**: Drink lots of fluids with breakfast (even coffee).
- **Before starting on the trail**: Top off the tank by drinking additional fluids.
- **On the trail**: Drink at every rest stop or break *even if you are not thirsty*.
- **Dehydration symptoms**: If your mouth is dry and sticky, significant dehydration has already begun. Immediately stop and drink fluids even if it seems inconvenient.
- **Lunch**: Have foods with water in them such as soups and drink more water.
- **Mid-day rest**: Spend some time after lunch resting so the water can be processed by your system.
- **Dinner**: Take time to drink small amounts of water over a period of several hours so your body tissues will rehydrate.

According to a large body of research, absolutely the best fluid to drink to remain hydrated is water. That's right, just plain water. Water is better than coffee, tea, and sports drinks in spite of all the advertising. On the trail, drink water and save the other beverages for meals and around camp.

Snacks and GORP

"Earl: Nelson and I are taking a little hike, so I'm making us a bag of trail mix.

Opal: Trail mix? What are you putting in it?

Earl: Oh, the usual…granola, peanuts, Chex cereal, raisins, M&M's…

Opal: (Looking into the bag.): And what are those little white things?

Earl: Rolaids."

"Pickles©" comic strip by Brian Crane

There are several anecdotal explanations of origin of the word 'GORP'. One of the most common is that it's an acronym for **G**ood **O**ld **R**aisins and **P**eanuts. Another translation is **G**ranola, **O**ats, **R**aisins and **P**eanuts. Take your pick or make up your own.

Today, GORP or trail mix is a general term that refers to snack foods used to keep energy levels up during the long hours between meals while doing heavy outdoor exercise. The goal of snacking is to consume calories throughout the day that will be converted to energy for muscles to do work. This avoids the feast or famine highs and lows that result from eating two or three large meals per day with nothing between. Snacks should be available for everyone at every rest stop. On the trail, food is not just something nice to have at a rest stop. Eating high calorie snacks to keep energy levels up is as important as staying adequately hydrated.

Insufficient calories will significantly reduce the ability of someone to participate in strenuous outdoor activities.

GORP Recipes

There are a number of recipes for various kinds of GORP and trail snacks and on a long trip a variety of different formulas should be available. Whichever recipe, here are some things to consider before whipping up a batch.

- Check with members of the party to determine if anyone has any food allergies, especially peanut allergies. Eliminate problem foods in the mix.

- Choose ingredients that are durable based on the nature of the trip and weather. Don't create a snack that will melt easily in hot weather, for example.

- Don't carry snack foods in the original small containers since the packaging could pose litter problems and the odor on the wrapper will attract animals.

- Pack snacks into reusable locking plastic bags for each person. For food safety, don't share a large communal bag.

There are as many recipes for GORP as there are people that mix them. Commercially prepared GORP is available, but it's expensive compared to homemade and tends (to my taste) to be overly sweet.

The problem with GORP is that after a few days everyone gets bored with it. On an extended trip, make up several totally different mixes to provide some variety. Listed below are some combinations I like. Some of these are a far cry from basic raisins and peanuts, but they are excellent. Experiment with different kinds and proportions of ingredients*.

---

* My GORP recipes tend to have a lot of peanut M&Ms® in them. Even if someone doesn't like the other ingredients, he or she will mine out the M&Ms® as if they were gold nuggets.

My Favorite GORP Recipe:

Seedless raisins, dry roasted peanuts, peanut *M&Ms®* and a semi-sweet cereal such as *Honey-nut Cheerios®*.

Classic:

Seedless raisins, peanuts and *M&Ms®*.

Classic Granola:

Raisins, peanuts, *M&Ms®* and granola cereal.

Sunny Days:

Dry roasted peanuts, roasted sunflower kernels, raisins and *M&Ms®* in equal amounts.

Fruit Cocktail:

Dried pineapple, apples, cherries and raisins.

Caribbean Punch:

Dried pineapple, coconut flakes, papaya, bananas and cashews.

Bedouin Desert Traveler:

Chopped dates, sliced almonds, pistachio nuts and coconut.

Saturday Morning TV:

Sweetened cereal with marshmallows, peanuts and raisins.

Sugar and Spice:

Sweetened oat squares cereal, miniature no-salt pretzels, brown sugar, a pinch of ground cinnamon and chopped dried fruit. Shake the bag.

George of the Jungle:

Dried banana chips, coconut, papaya and dried pineapple.

Yogi Bear's Jellystone Park:

Puffed corn cereal, honey-roasted peanuts, candy gummy bears and raisins.

I don't particularly like salty GORP combinations since they increase my thirst on the trail. They are nice for different tasting snacks at the end of the day. Here are a few salty combinations I have tried:

Bridge Club Mix:
Pretzels, mixed nuts, mixture of various flavors of *Chex®* cereal.
Friday Night at the Movies:
Popcorn (a variety of flavors; cheese is a favorite), peanuts and chocolate *M&Ms®*.
Airline Coach Class:
Small cheese-flavored crackers, raisins, pretzels, granola and a touch of coconut.
Fish and Rice:
Rice cakes, cheese 'fish' crackers, lots of raisins or dates and pretzels.

For food safety reasons, always prepare small locking plastic bags of GORP for each member of your party. *Never share a large common bag.*

Breads and Muffins

"Good bread is the most fundamentally satisfying of all foods; and good bread with fresh butter, the greatest of feasts."

James Beard

"Coleridge holds that a man cannot have a pure mind who refuses apple dumplings. I am not certain but he is right."

Charles Lamb

Writers have extolled the pleasures of bread for centuries. The process of mixing and kneading, the baking odor, its texture and flavor and even its final appearance at a meal are unlike any other food. Each variety of bread or muffin shares so many of the same traits yet each remains different and unique. Prepared outdoors, as part of a camp meal, breads and muffins move from the supporting role they have at home to one of the main players on the culinary stage. A wilderness chef can prepare bread as dumplings, in casseroles, fried like pancakes in a pan and in the Outback Oven.

The Outback Oven is the perfect cooking tool in which to bake breads and muffins. There are many inexpensive prepackaged mixes that can be prepared by just adding water and baking. These commercial mixes can be easily enhanced and many of the recipes in this collection use a prepackaged mix as a base to make something altogether different.

There are several things to consider when using the Outback Oven to make breads and muffins:

- Use only as much water as needed to make a very thick batter than can be just spread in the pan. Too much water lengthens the baking time significantly. If a recipe is not getting done in the time indicated, there may be too much water in the batter.

- Stir and stir and stir and then stir some more, before adding more water. Some recipes require a lot of stirring before all the dry ingredients are well mixed and moist.

- If more water is needed add only a teaspoon at a time and then stir again. It's easy to add too much.

- Keep the temperature in the middle of the "Bake" range on the thermometer. Increasing the temperature doesn't speed up baking. The bottom of the bread just burns. Be patient, monitor the thermometer frequently and adjust the flame (usually down) as needed.

- I don't normally separate biscuits and muffins in the pan, so technically they are breads. They taste the same and it's much less work. Just spread the batter over the bottom of the pan and bake. After it's done, cut it into serving size pieces.

- Don't skip the standing time. Almost all of the bread and muffin recipes require at least 5 minutes of standing time. The term "Let stand" means to extinguish the stove flame and let the Oven and its contents stand with the dome over the pan for the time required.

- Eat the bread or muffins right away; they are much better warm. Generally the finished product will not be as good after sitting for hours.

If you've never used an Outback Oven to make camp baked goods, it's time to try. The recipes here are simple to prepare and add so much to a meal. I've used one for about 7 or 8 years and can't imagine preparing trails meals without it.

Anadama Bread

In the first plastic bag, mix together:

- 1½ cups all-purpose flour
- ½ cup cornmeal muffin mix
- 2 tablespoons dried egg
- ½ teaspoon salt
- 1 teaspoon sugar
- 1 tablespoon baking powder
- ½ tablespoon baking soda

Carry separately:

- ¼ cup molasses

Preparation:

- Mix 1 cup water with the contents of the *first bag* in the Outback Oven pan.
- Stir in molasses and mix until well blended.
- Assemble the Oven and bake 12 minutes. Let stand 5 minutes before serving.

Notes:

Apple Loaf

In the first plastic bag, mix together:

- 2 cups all-purpose flour
- 1 cup white sugar
- 3 tablespoons dried egg
- 1 teaspoon baking powder
- ½ teaspoon baking soda
- ¼ teaspoon ground cinnamon
- ½ teaspoon salt
- ½ cup chopped nuts (optional)

Carry separately:

- ½ cup dried apples, chopped
- 1 teaspoon vanilla extract

Preparation:

- Mix 1¼ cup water with apples in the Outback Oven pan.
- Set pan directly on stove and bring to a boil.
- Remove from heat, cover and let stand 5 minutes.
- Mix in the contents of the *first bag* and the vanilla.
- Assemble the Oven and bake 14 minutes.

Notes:

Apricot Bread with a Touch of Chocolate

In the first plastic bag, mix together:

- 2 cups all-purpose flour
- ¾ cup sugar
- 1 tablespoon baking powder
- ¼ teaspoon baking soda
- 2 tablespoons powdered milk
- 2 tablespoons dried egg
- 1 cup dried apricots, chopped (substitute peaches)
- ¼ cup semisweet chocolate chips
- ¼ cup chopped nuts, chopped (optional)

Preparation:

- Mix 1¼ cup water with the contents of the *first bag* in the Outback Oven pan.
- Stir until well blended.
- Assemble the Oven and bake 14 minutes. Let stand 5 minutes.

Notes:

Apricot Swirl Bread

In the first plastic bag, mix together:

- 1 package apple-cinnamon muffin mix (8 ounces; 1¾ cups)
- 2 tablespoons dried egg
- 2 tablespoons powdered milk
- ½ teaspoon ground cinnamon
- 1 tablespoon brown sugar

Carry separately:

- ¼ cup apricot preserves (or peach)
- ½ cup powdered sugar for topping (optional)

Preparation:

- Mix ½ cup water with the contents of the *first bag* in the Outback Oven pan.
- Stir well and spread across the bottom of the pan.
- Squeeze out apricot preserves in lumps on batter. Cut across lines with a knife.
- Assemble the Oven and bake 12 minutes.
- Shake powdered sugar on top.

Notes:

Baking Powder Biscuits

In the first plastic bag, mix together:

- 2 cups all-purpose flour
- 1 tablespoon baking powder
- ½ cup powdered milk
- ½ teaspoon salt

Carry separately:

- ¼ cup margarine

Preparation:

- Mix the margarine with the contents of the *first bag* in the Outback Oven pan.
- Using a knife, cut in margarine until the mixture is crumbly.
- Stir in ¾ cup water and mix until well blended and no longer dry.
- Spread batter over the bottom of the pan or separate into single biscuits.
- Assemble the Oven and bake 9 minutes.

Notes:

Banana Bran Muffins

In the first plastic bag, mix together:

- 1 package bran with dates muffin mix (8 ounces; 1¾ cups)
- ½ cup brown sugar
- 2 tablespoons dried egg
- ¼ cup powdered milk
- 2 tablespoons nuts, finely chopped

Carry separately:

- 1 very ripe banana (one with a lot of small brown spots on the peel)

Preparation:

- Mash the banana with a fork in Outback Oven pan.
- Add ¾ cup water and contents of the *first bag* and mix well.
- Assemble the Oven and bake 12 minutes.

Notes:

Bannock Bread

In the first plastic bag, mix together:

- 2 cups all-purpose flour
- 2 tablespoons sugar
- ½ cup powdered milk
- ½ teaspoon salt
- 1 teaspoon baking powder
- ½ teaspoon baking soda
- 1 tablespoon dried egg
- 1 cup raisins

Preparation:

- Mix 1 cup water with the contents of the *first bag* in the Outback Oven pan.
- Stir until well blended.
- Assemble the Oven and bake 10 minutes.

Notes:

Bee Hive Muffins

In the first plastic bag, mix together:

- 1 package bran or bran with dates muffin mix (8 ounces; 1¾ cups)
- ¼ cup brown sugar
- 2 tablespoons dried egg
- ¼ cup powdered milk
- ¼ cup raisins

Carry separately:

- 3 tablespoons honey (or more to taste)

Preparation:

- Mix 1/2 cup water with the contents of the *first bag* in the Outback Oven pan.
- Add honey and stir until well blended.
- Assemble the Oven and bake 10 minutes. Let stand 3-5 minutes.

Notes:

Big Daddy's Biscuits

In the first plastic bag, mix together:

- 2 cups all-purpose flour
- 1 tablespoon baking powder
- 1 teaspoon salt
- 1 tablespoon white sugar
- ½ cup powdered milk
- 1 tablespoon non-dairy coffee creamer

Carry separately:

- ½ cup margarine

Preparation:

- Mix the margarine with the contents of the *first bag* in the Outback Oven pan.
- Using a knife, cut the margarine in until the mixture is crumbly.
- Stir in ¾ cup water and mix well.
- Spread the batter over the Oven pan or separate into individual biscuits.
- Assemble the Oven and bake 9 minutes.

Notes:

Bran Flakes Muffins with Raisins

In the first plastic bag, mix together:

- 1 cup bran flakes cereal with raisins, slightly crushed
- ½ cup powdered milk

In the second plastic bag, mix together:

- 1 cup all-purpose flour
- 2 tablespoons dried egg
- ¼ cup raisins
- 2½ teaspoons baking powder
- ¼ cup sugar
- ½ teaspoon salt

Preparation:

- Mix ¾ cup water with the contents of the *first bag* in the Outback Oven pan.
- Cover and let stand 2-3 minutes until mixture is moistened.
- Mix in the contents of the *second bag* and stir until well blended.
- Assemble the Oven and bake 10 minutes.

Notes:

Bran-Molasses Bread

In the first plastic bag, mix together:

- 1 package bran or bran with dates muffin mix (8 ounces; 1¾ cups)
- 1 tablespoon dried egg
- 2 tablespoons powdered milk
- ¼ cup raisins
- 1 tablespoon brown sugar

Carry separately:

- 2 tablespoons molasses

Preparation:

- Mix ½ cup water with the contents of the *first bag* in the Outback Oven pan.
- Stir in molasses and mix until well blended.
- Assemble the Oven and bake 10 minutes.

Notes:

Buttermilk Biscuits

In the first plastic bag, mix together:

- 2 cups *self-rising* flour (no substitutes)
- 2 teaspoons white sugar
- 1 teaspoon baking powder
- ½ cup powdered buttermilk mix
- ¼ teaspoon salt

Carry separately:

- ½ cup margarine

Preparation:

- Mix the contents of the *first bag* with the margarine in the Outback Oven pan.
- Using a knife cut in margarine until the mixture is crumbly.
- Stir in ¾ cup water and mix until the ingredients are no longer dry.
- Spread batter over the bottom of the pan or separate into single biscuits.
- Assemble the Oven and bake 10 minutes.

Notes:

Cake Style Cornbread

In the first plastic bag, mix together:

- 1 cup all-purpose baking mix
- 1 package cornmeal muffin mix (8 ounces; 1¾ cups)
- ¼ cup sugar
- 4 teaspoons dried egg
- ¼ cup powdered milk

Carry separately:

- 1 teaspoon vanilla

Preparation:

- Mix ¾ cup water with the contents of the *first bag* in the Outback Oven pan.
- Stir in vanilla.
- Assemble the Oven and bake 12 minutes. Let stand 5 minutes.

Notes:

Camp Cornbread

In the first plastic bag, mix together:

- 1 can home-dried corn (15 ounces)

In the second plastic bag, mix together:

- 1 package cornbread muffin mix (8 ounces; 1¾ cups)
- ¼ cup powdered milk
- 2 tablespoons dry egg
- 1 tablespoons non-dairy coffee creamer
- ¼ cup sugar

Preparation:

- Mix ¾ cup water with the contents of the *first bag* in the Outback Oven pan.
- Set pan directly on the stove and bring to a boil.
- Reduce heat, cover and simmer 6 minutes.
- Remove from the stove, cover and let stand 5 minutes. Don't skip this step.
- Mix in the contents of the *second bag*. Blend well.
- Assemble the Oven and bake 12 minutes. Let stand 5 minutes.

Notes:

Cheese Temptation Bread

In the first plastic bag, mix together:

- 1½ cups all-purpose baking mix
- 1 tablespoon dried egg
- ¼ teaspoon salt
- 1 cup cornflakes or other unsweetened flake cold cereal
- ½ cup shredded sharp cheddar cheese (4 ounces)

Preparation:

- Mix ½ cup water with the contents of the *first bag* in the Outback Oven pan.
- Blend well.
- Assemble the Oven and bake 10 minutes.

Notes:

Cherry Nut Bread

In the first plastic bag, mix together:

- 1¾ cups all-purpose baking mix
- ½ cup sugar
- 2 tablespoons dried egg
- ¼ cup chopped nuts
- ¾ cup dried cherries

Carry separately:

- ¼ cup powdered sugar for topping (optional)

Preparation:

- Mix ½ cup water with the contents of the *first bag* in the Outback Oven.
- Assemble the Oven and bake 12 minutes. Let stand 5 minutes.
- Shake powdered sugar on top.

Notes:

Cherry Spice Loaf

In the first plastic bag, mix together:

- 1½ cups all-purpose flour
- ¾ cup sugar
- ¼ cup powdered milk
- 1½ teaspoons baking powder
- ½ teaspoon baking soda
- ¼ teaspoon salt

In the second plastic bag, mix together:

- ¼ cup raisins
- ½ cup dry cherries
- ¼ cup chopped nuts
- ¼ dates chopped (optional)

Carry separately:

- 1 teaspoon almond extract

Preparation:

- Mix ¾ cup water with the contents of the *first bag* in the Outback Oven pan.
- Stir in the contents of the *second bag*. Add almond extract.
- Stir only enough to moisten all ingredients.
- Assemble the Oven and bake 12 minutes. Let stand 5 minutes.

Notes:

Chocolate Raisin Oatmeal Muffins

In the first plastic bag, mix together:

- 1 cup all-purpose flour
- 1 cup quick cooking oats
- ¼ cup powdered milk
- 2 tablespoons dried egg
- 1 tablespoon baking powder
- 2 tablespoons unsweetened cocoa powder (not hot chocolate mix)
- ½ cup sugar
- ¼ teaspoon salt

Carry separately:

- ½ cup raisins

Preparation:

- Mix ¾ cup water with the contents of the *first bag* in the Outback Oven pan.
- Stir in raisins and mix until ingredients are no longer dry.
- Assemble the Oven and bake 12 minutes.

Notes:

Cinnamon Sour Cream Biscuits

In the first plastic bag, mix together:

- 2 cups all-purpose flour
- ¼ cup raisins
- 2 tablespoons white sugar
- 2 teaspoons baking powder
- ¼ teaspoon baking soda
- ¼ teaspoon salt
- ½ teaspoon ground cinnamon
- 2 tablespoon powdered milk
- 2 tablespoons dry sour cream mix (substitute 1 tablespoon lemon juice)

Carry separately:

- ½ cup margarine
- ½ cup powdered sugar for topping (don't skip this)

Preparation:

- Mix the contents of the *first bag* with the margarine in the Outback Oven pan.
- Using a knife cut in margarine until the mixture is crumbly.
- Stir in 1 cup water and mix until ingredients are no longer dry.
- Spread over the bottom of the Oven pan.
- Using a knife separate the batter into single biscuits.
- Assemble the Oven and bake 12 minutes.
- Shake the powdered sugar on top.

Notes:

Confetti Cornbread

In the first plastic bag, mix together:

- 1 can home-dried corn with red and green peppers

In the second plastic bag, mix together:

- 1 package cornbread muffin mix (8 ounces; 1¾ cups)
- 2 tablespoons dried egg
- ¼ cup powdered milk
- 1 teaspoon sugar
- ½ teaspoon salt

Preparation:

- Mix 1 cup water with the contents of the *first bag* in the Outback Oven pan.
- Set pan directly on the stove and bring to a boil.
- Reduce heat, cover and simmer 6 minutes.
- Remove from the stove and let stand 5 minutes. Don't skip this step.
- Stir in the contents of the *second bag* and mix well.
- Add small amounts of water, if necessary, to get a very thick batter.
- Assemble the Oven and bake 12 minutes.

Notes:

County Fair Cornbread

In the first plastic bag, mix together:

- ½ cup cornmeal muffin mix
- 1 cup all-purpose flour
- ½ cup sugar
- 1 tablespoon baking powder
- ½ cup powdered milk
- 4 tablespoons dried egg
- 1 teaspoon salt

Carry separately:

- 1 teaspoon vanilla extract

Preparation:

- Mix ¾ cup water with the contents of the *first bag* in the Outback Oven pan.
- Stir in vanilla and spread the batter over the bottom of the pan.
- Assemble the Oven and bake 10 minutes. Let stand 5 minutes.

Notes:

Cranberry Loaf

In the first plastic bag, mix together:

- 1 cup all-purpose flour
- 1 cup graham cracker crumbs
- 2 teaspoons baking powder
- 1 tablespoon sugar
- ½ teaspoon salt
- 2 tablespoons dried egg

In the second plastic bag, mix together:

- ½ cup raisins
- ½ cup dry cranberries, chopped

Preparation:

- Mix 1 cup water with the contents of the *first bag* in the Outback Oven pan.
- Stir until well blended.
- Mix in the contents of the *second bag*.
- Assemble the Oven and bake 12 minutes.

Notes:

Easy Butter Biscuits

In the first plastic bag, mix together:

- 2 cups *self-rising* flour (no substitutes)
- ¼ cup powdered buttermilk
- 1 tablespoon sugar
- 1 tablespoon dried egg

Carry separately:

- ½ cup margarine

Preparation:

- Mix the contents of the *first bag* with the margarine in the Outback Oven pan.
- Add margarine and using a knife, cut the butter in until the mixture is crumbly.
- Stir in ½ cup water and mix until ingredients are no longer dry.
- Spread batter over the bottom of the pan, or separate into single biscuits.
- Assemble the Oven and bake 10 minutes.

Notes:

German Pancake

In the first plastic bag, mix together:

- 1 cup all-purpose flour
- 1 package dried egg (6 ounces)
- ½ cup powdered milk
- 2 tablespoons powdered buttermilk
- 2 tablespoon brown sugar

In the second plastic bag, mix together:

- ½ cup powdered sugar for topping

Preparation:

- Mix 1½ cups water with the contents of the *first bag* in the Outback Oven pan.
- Keep stirring until batter is smooth.
- Assemble the Oven and bake 14 minutes. Let stand 5 minutes.
- Add 2 teaspoons water to the contents of the *second bag*. Mix by squeezing the bag. Cut a small hole in the corner and drizzle over the pancake.

Notes:

Graham Cracker Raisin Loaf

In the first plastic bag, mix together:

- 1 cup all-purpose flour
- 1 cup graham cracker crumbs
- ½ cup brown sugar, packed
- 2 tablespoons powdered milk
- 2 tablespoons dried egg
- 2 teaspoons baking powder

In the second plastic bag, mix together:

- ½ cup raisins
- ¼ cup chopped nuts (optional)

Preparation:

- Mix ¾ cup water with the contents of the *first bag* in the Outback Oven pan.
- Stir in the contents of the *second bag* and stir until well blended.
- Assemble the Oven and bake 12 minutes.

Notes:

Hazelnut Scones

In the first plastic bag, mix together:

- 2 cups all-purpose flour
- ¼ cup brown sugar, packed
- ¼ cup chopped hazelnuts (or almonds)
- 2 teaspoons baking powder
- ½ teaspoon ground cardamom
- ¼ teaspoon salt
- 2 tablespoons dried egg
- 2 tablespoons powdered buttermilk

Carry separately:

- ½ cup margarine

Preparation:

- Mix the contents of the *first bag* with the margarine in the Outback Oven pan.
- Using a knife, cut the margarine in until the mixture is crumbly.
- Stir in ¾ cup water and mix until ingredients are no longer dry.
- Assemble the Oven and bake 12 minutes. Let stand 5 minutes.

Notes:

Honey Cornbread

In the first plastic bag, mix together:

- 1 cup all-purpose flour
- 1 cup yellow cornmeal muffin mix
- ¼ cup sugar
- 1 teaspoon baking powder
- 3 tablespoons non-dairy coffee creamer
- 4 tablespoons dried egg

Carry separately:

- ¼ cup honey

Preparation:

- Mix ¾ cup water with the contents of the *first bag* in the Outback Oven pan.
- Stir in honey and mix until well blended.
- Assemble the Oven and bake 12 minutes. Let stand 5 minutes.

Notes:

Irish Soda Bread

In the first plastic bag, mix together:

- 1½ cups all-purpose flour
- ¼ cup sugar
- 2 tablespoons dried egg
- ½ teaspoon baking powder
- 2 teaspoons baking soda
- ½ teaspoon salt
- ¼ cup powdered buttermilk

Preparation:

- Mix ¾ cup plus 2 tablespoons water with the contents of the *first bag* in the Outback Oven pan.
- Stir until well blended.
- Assemble the Oven and bake 12 minutes. Let stand 5 minutes.

Notes:

Italian Parmesan Bread

In the first plastic bag, mix together:

- 1 package pizza dough mix (6-7 ounces)
- ¾ cup all-purpose flour
- 2 tablespoons dried egg
- 1 tablespoon Italian or pizza spice
- ½ cup grated Parmesan cheese

Carry separately:

- ¼ cup French fried onions (optional)

Preparation:

- Mix 1 cup water with the contents of the *first bag* in the Outback Oven pan.
- Stir until well blended.
- Spread onions on top of batter.
- Assemble the Oven and bake 10 minutes. Let stand 5 minutes.

Notes:

Morning Glory Muffins

In the first plastic bag, mix together:

- 1¼ cup all-purpose flour
- ¼ cup graham cracker crumbs
- ¾ cup sugar
- 4 tablespoons dried egg
- 1 teaspoon ground cinnamon
- 1 tablespoon baking powder
- ½ tablespoon baking soda
- ½ cup chopped nuts (optional)

In the second plastic bag, mix together:

- ¼ cup dried apple (or other dried fruit), chopped
- ¼ cup raisins

Carry separately:

- 1 tablespoon vanilla extract

Preparation:

- Mix ¾ cup water with the contents of the *first bag* in the Outback Oven pan.
- Stir until the ingredients are just moistened. Stir in vanilla.
- Mix in the contents of the *second bag*. Stir until well blended.
- Assemble the Oven and bake 14 minutes. Let stand 5 minutes.

Notes:

Oatmeal Bread

In the first plastic bag, mix together:

- 1½ cups all-purpose flour
- ¾ cup quick cooking oats
- ¼ cup raisins
- 1 tablespoon sugar
- 1 teaspoon baking powder
- ¼ cup powdered buttermilk

Carry separately:

- ½ cup powdered sugar for topping

Preparation:

- Mix ¾ cup water with the contents of the *first bag* in the Outback Oven pan.
- Stir well and spread evenly over the bottom of the pan.
- Assemble the Oven and bake 12 minutes. Let stand 5 minutes.
- Add 2 teaspoons water to the powdered sugar and mix by squeezing the bag. Cut a hole in the corner of the bag and drizzle over the bread.

Notes:

Peanut Butter Loaf

In the first plastic bag, mix together:

- 1¼ cups all-purpose flour
- ½ cup brown sugar, packed
- 2 tablespoons dry egg
- ¼ cup powdered buttermilk
- 1 teaspoon baking soda
- ½ teaspoon salt

Carry separately:

- 1 teaspoon vanilla extract
- ¼ cup smooth peanut butter

Preparation:

- Mix ½ cup water with the contents of the *first bag* in the Outback Oven pan.
- Stir in vanilla and peanut butter. Mix well before adding any more water.
- Assemble the Oven and bake 14 minutes. Let stand 10 minutes.

Notes:

Poppy Seed Muffins

In the first plastic bag, mix together:

- 1¾ cups all-purpose baking mix
- ½ cup sugar
- 1 tablespoon poppy or other small seeds (optional)
- ¾ cup raisins
- 2 tablespoons dried egg
- ¼ cup powdered buttermilk (plain powdered milk will work)

Carry separately:

- 1 tablespoon lemon juice
- 1 teaspoon vanilla extract

Preparation:

- Mix ½ cup water with the contents of the *first bag* in the Outback Oven pan.
- Sir in lemon juice and vanilla. Mix until well blended.
- Assemble the Oven and bake 12 minutes. Let stand 5 minutes.

Notes:

Raisin Bread

In the first plastic bag, mix together:

- 1¾ cups all-purpose flour
- ¼ cup cornmeal
- 2 tablespoons dark brown sugar
- ¼ cup raisins
- ¼ cup powdered milk
- 1 tablespoon baking powder
- ½ teaspoon salt
- ½ teaspoon baking soda

Carry separately:

- ¼ cup honey

Preparation:

- Mix 1 cup water with the contents of the *first bag* in the Outback Oven pan.
- Stir in honey and spread batter evenly over the bottom of the pan.
- Assemble the Oven and bake 12 minutes. Let stand 5 minutes.

Notes:

Raisin Nut Bread

In the first plastic bag, mix together:

- 2 cups all-purpose flour
- ¾ cup sugar
- 2 tablespoons dried egg
- 1 tablespoon baking powder
- ½ teaspoon baking soda
- ¾ teaspoon ground cinnamon
- ½ cup raisins
- ¼ cup chopped nuts

Preparation:

- Mix ¾ cup water with the contents of the *first bag* in the Outback Oven pan.
- Stir until well blended.
- Assemble the Oven and bake 15 minutes. Let stand 5 minutes.

Notes:

Red Pepper Biscuits

In the first plastic bag, mix together:

- 1¾ cups all-purpose baking mix
- ½ cup powdered milk
- ½ teaspoon garlic powder
- ½ teaspoon red pepper flakes

Carry separately:

- ½ cup shredded cheddar cheese

Preparation:

- Mix ¾ cup water with the contents of the *first bag* in the Outback Oven pan.
- Stir in cheese.
- Spread the batter over the Oven pan or separate into individual biscuits.
- Assemble the Oven and bake 12 minutes. Let stand 5 minutes.

Notes:

Smooth Southern Biscuits

In the first plastic bag, mix together:

- 2 cups *self-rising* flour (no substitutes)
- ¼ cup powdered buttermilk

Carry separately:

- 3 individual serving size packages of mayonnaise (about 3 tablespoons)
- 2 tablespoons vegetable oil

Preparation:

- Mix ¾ cup water with the contents of the *first bag* in the Outback Oven pan.
- Stir in mayonnaise and oil.
- Mix until all ingredients are no longer dry.
- Spread over the Oven pan or separate into individual biscuits.
- Assemble the Oven and bake 12 minutes. Let stand 5 minutes.

Notes:

Southern Sweet Potato Bread with Pecans

In the first plastic bag, mix together:

- 1½ cups all-purpose flour
- ¾ cup sugar
- 2 tablespoons dried egg
- 2 teaspoons baking powder
- 1 teaspoon nutmeg
- ½ teaspoon ground cinnamon
- ¼ teaspoon salt
- 1 tablespoon powdered milk
- ¼ cup chopped pecans

Carry separately:

- ½ cup home-dried sweet potatoes
- ¼ cup raisins

Preparation:

- Mix 1 cup water with the sweet potatoes in the Outback Oven pan.
- Set pan directly on the stove and bring to a boil.
- Reduce heat and simmer 5-7 minutes. Remove from the stove, cover and let stand 5 minutes.
- Mash sweet potatoes. Mix in the contents of the *first bag*.
- Stir in raisins. Add small amounts of water, if needed.
- Assemble the Oven and bake 14 minutes. Let stand 5 minutes.

Notes:

Strawberry Bread

In the first plastic bag, mix together:

- 1½ cups all-purpose flour
- ¾ cup sugar
- 3 tablespoons dry egg
- 1 teaspoon ground cinnamon
- 1 teaspoon baking powder
- ½ teaspoon salt
- ¼ teaspoon baking soda

Carry separately:

- ½ cup strawberry jam or preserves
- 1 tablespoon vegetable oil
- ½ cup powdered sugar (optional for topping)

Preparation:

- Mix ¾ cup water with the contents of the *first bag* in the Outback Oven pan.
- Stir in vegetable oil and mix until well blended.
- Drop strawberry jam by the spoonful on top. Swirl with a knife.
- Assemble the Oven and bake 14 minutes. Let stand 5 minutes.
- Sprinkle powdered sugar on the bread or make glaze by adding two teaspoons water to the sugar.

Notes:

Waikiki Cornbread

In the first plastic bag, mix together:

- 1½ cups all-purpose baking mix
- ¾ cup sugar
- ¼ cup cornmeal muffin mix
- 2 teaspoons baking powder
- 2 tablespoons dried egg
- 2 tablespoons powdered buttermilk

Carry separately:

- ¼ cup pineapple jam or preserves (substitute orange marmalade)

Preparation:

- Mix 1 cup water with the contents of the *first bag* in the Outback Oven pan.
- Stir until all ingredients are no longer dry.
- Mix in jam or preserves.
- Assemble the Oven and bake 15 minutes. Let stand 5 minutes.

Notes:

Welsh Bread

In the first plastic bag, mix together:

- 1½ cups all-purpose flour
- ¼ cup powdered milk
- 2 tablespoons dried egg
- 2 tablespoons dark brown sugar
- 2 teaspoons baking powder
- 1 teaspoon baking soda
- ¼ teaspoon salt
- ½ cup raisins

Carry separately:

- 2 tablespoons molasses (full flavor)

Preparation:

- Mix ¾ cup water with the contents of the *first bag* in the Outback Oven.
- Stir in molasses.
- Assemble the Oven and bake 14 minutes. Let stand 5 minutes.

Notes:

Outback Oven Recipes

"…a good dinner is of great importance to good talk. One cannot think well, love well, sleep well, if one has not dined well."

Virginia Woolf

I can't think of a cooking tool developed in the last few years that has changed wilderness cooking more than the Outback Oven. This clever, lightweight device allows a wilderness chef to prepare on the trail just about anything that can be baked at home. In addition, it's versatile because the pans can be used to prepare other meals. Often, this is the only set of pans I carry on weekend trips. Preparing a recipe using the Outback Oven requires about 1/3 less fuel than preparing the same recipe using a conventional pan, and it requires less attention from the chef once the Oven is set up.

Detailed instructions on how to use the Oven can be found in Chapter Two. Although it's relatively easy to use, some practice is required. I definitely recommend that the inexperienced chef practice and prepare the same recipes that will be used on a trip before heading out on the trail.

Some additional suggestions about using the Oven to prepare main meals include:

- All recipes have been prepared using the 10-inch Outback Oven.

- Many recipes require that the items in a commercial mix be divided. That is, only part of the mix is used in the recipe such as using only the dry potatoes from a scalloped potato mix, but not the sauce packets. The leftover sauce packets can be mixed with a little water and vegetables to make flavorful side dishes or they can be used in other recipes. Read the home preparation directions carefully.

- Most recipes require that, after mixing with water, the mixture must be brought to a full boil before baking in the Oven. Boiling brings the food up to cooking temperature quicker so food gets done faster. It also saves fuel.

- Baking time begins when the temperature first reaches the low end of the "Bake" range on the thermometer.

- Try to keep the temperature just above the middle of the "Bake" range.

- In warm weather, use a windscreen if there is any significant air movement and always use one, wind or not, in the winter to help trap heat around the Oven. Keep the detached fuel bottle outside of the windscreen.

- If the recipe instructions require the pan to stand for a few minutes, don't remove the pan from the stove. Turn the stove off and let it stand with the convection dome over the pan.

The Outback Oven opens a whole new world of outdoor recipes. It can be used to make breads, muffins, casseroles, desserts and almost anything that can be made in an oven at home. Now many favorite baked recipes made at home can be adapted and prepared outdoors. With a little imagination, the opportunities for creative camp baking are endless.

Beef Stew and Biscuits

This recipe absolutely fills the Outback Oven. Be sure to cook on a solid level surface and handle the Oven carefully to prevent spills.

In the first plastic bag, mix together:
- 1 package *Wyler's Soup Starter Hearty Beef Stew*® mix
- ½ cup TVP beef chunk style
- 1 can home-dried vegetables

In the second plastic bag mix together:
- 1 package of biscuit mix (8 ounces)
- 1 tablespoon dried egg

Preparation:
- Mix 3½ cups water and the contents of the *first bag* in the Outback Oven pan.
- Bring to a boil, cover and simmer 5-6 minutes.
- Remove from heat and cover. Let stand 5 minutes.
- Pour ½ cup water into the *second bag*. Mix by squeezing the bag.
- Cut a hole in the corner of the bag. Squeeze out lumps of batter on top of stew.
- Assemble the Oven and bake 14 minutes. Let stand 5 minutes.

Notes:

Beef Tamale Squares

In the first plastic bag, mix together:

- 1 cup ground beef style TVP
- 1 tablespoon instant beef-flavor bouillon
- 1 tablespoon chili powder (more or less to taste)
- 1 can home-dried corn with red and green peppers
- ½ cup home-dried or sun-dried tomatoes (optional)

In the second plastic bag, mix together:

- 1 package cornbread muffin mix (8 ounces)
- ¼ cup powdered milk
- 4 tablespoons dried egg

Carry separately:

- ¼ cup shredded cheddar cheese

Preparation:

- Mix 2½ cups water with the contents of the *first bag* in the Outback Oven pan.
- Set pan directly on the stove and bring to a boil. Simmer 5-7 minutes or until the corn is tender.
- Remove from heat. Stir in the contents of the *second bag* and mix well.
- Spread cheese on top.
- Assemble the Oven and bake 12 minutes. Let stand 5 minutes.

Notes:

Cheesy Corn and Bacon Bake

In the first plastic bag, mix together:

- 4 tablespoons bacon bits (not the real meat kind)
- 2 cans home-dried corn with red and green peppers

In the second plastic bag, mix together:

- ¾ cup all-purpose baking mix
- ½ cup powdered milk
- 4 tablespoons dry egg
- 1/8 teaspoon black pepper

Carry separately:

- ¼ cup grated Parmesan cheese

Preparation:

- Mix ¾ cup water with the contents of the *first bag* in the Outback Oven pan.
- Set pan directly on the stove and bring to a boil.
- Reduce heat, cover and simmer gently 5 minutes.
- Remove from heat and let stand 5 minutes. Don't skip this step.
- Pour ½ cup water into the *second bag* and mix by squeezing.
- Pour over the top of the corn mixture in the pan. Shake cheese on top.
- Assemble the Oven and bake 10 minutes. Let stand 3 to 5 minutes.

Notes:

Chicken in French Onion Sauce

In the first plastic bag, mix together:

- 1 cup poultry chunk style TVP
- Envelope onion-flavored dry soup mix
- 1 tablespoon chicken-flavored bouillon
- 1 can home-dried carrots
- 1 can home-dried mushrooms (4½ ounces)
- ½ teaspoon celery salt
- ½ teaspoon garlic powder
- 1/8 teaspoon black pepper

Carry separately:

- 1 cup French fried onions
- ½ cup instant rice

Preparation:

- Mix 2½ cups water with the contents of the *first bag* in the Outback Oven pan.
- Set pan directly on the stove and bring to a boil.
- Reduce heat, cover and simmer 5 minutes.
- Remove from heat and stir in instant rice. Spread onions on top.
- Assemble the Oven and bake 10 minutes. Let stand 3 minutes.

Notes:

Chicken Puff

In the first plastic bag, mix together:

- 1 cup poultry style chunk TVP
- 1 tablespoon chicken-flavored bouillon
- 1 can home-dried carrots

In the second plastic bag, mix together:

- 1½ cups all-purpose flour
- ¼ cup powdered milk
- 3 tablespoons dried egg
- 2 teaspoons baking powder
- ½ teaspoon salt

Preparation:

- Mix 2 cups water with the contents of the *first bag* in the Outback Oven pan.
- Set pan directly on the stove and bring to a boil. Reduce heat and simmer 5 minutes.
- Remove from heat and stir in ½ cup cold water and contents of the *second bag.*
- Stir until well blended.
- Assemble the Oven and bake 12 minutes. Let stand 5 minutes.

Notes:

Cornbread and Beef Casserole

In the first plastic bag, mix together:
- 1 cup ground beef style TVP
- 1 tablespoon beef-flavored bouillon
- 1 can home-dried corn
- 1 tablespoon dry onion

In the second plastic bag, mix together:
- 1 package cornbread muffin mix (8 ounces; 1¾ cups)
- 2 tablespoons dried egg
- ¼ cup powdered milk
- 2 tablespoons non-dairy coffee creamer

Carry separately:
- ½ cup shredded cheddar cheese

Preparation:
- Mix 2 cups water with the contents of the *first bag* in the Outback Oven pan.
- Set pan directly on the stove and bring to a boil.
- Reduce heat, cover and simmer 5 minutes. Remove from heat. Let stand 5 minutes.
- Add ½ cup cold water and stir in the contents of the *second bag.*
- Mix well. Shake cheese over the top.
- Assemble the Oven and bake 12 minutes. Let stand 5 minutes.

Notes:

Country Chicken and Cornbread

In the first plastic bag, mix together:

- 1½ cups poultry chunk style TVP
- 2 tablespoons chicken-flavored bouillon
- 1 can home-dried peas

In the second plastic bag, mix together:

- 1 package cornbread muffin mix (8 ounces; 1¾ cups)
- 1 tablespoon dry egg mix
- ¼ cup powdered milk

Carry separately:

- 1 envelope country gravy mix (makes 2 cups)

Preparation:

- Mix 2 cups water with the contents of the *first bag* in the Outback Oven pan.
- Bring to a boil, reduce heat and simmer 5 minutes.
- Remove from heat and mix in 1 cup cold water.
- Add the gravy mix and stir until well blended.
- Pour ¾ cup water into the *second bag* and mix by squeezing the bag.
- Spread over the mixture in the Oven pan.
- Assemble the Oven and bake 10 minutes. Let stand 3 to 5 minutes

Notes:

Country Sausage and Biscuits

In the first plastic bag, mix together:
- 1 cup ground beef style TVP
- 1 tablespoon instant beef-flavored bouillon
- 1 envelope country gravy mix with sausage (makes 2 cups)
- ½ cup powdered milk

In the second plastic bag, mix together:
- 1 package biscuit mix (8 ounces; 1½ cups)
- 1 tablespoon dried egg
- ¼ cup powdered milk or powdered buttermilk

Preparation:
- Mix 2½ cups water with the contents of the *first bag* in the Outback Oven pan.
- Set pan directly on the stove and bring to a boil. Simmer 3-4 minutes.
- Stir constantly. When it begins to thicken, remove from heat and cover.
- Pour ½ cup water into the *second bag*. Mix by squeezing the bag.
- Add small amounts of water, if needed, to get a batter that will just pour.
- Spread the batter over mix in the Oven pan.
- Assemble the Oven and bake 10 minutes. Let stand 3 to 5 minutes.

Notes:

Couscous Garden Pie

In the first plastic bag, mix together:

- 1 can home-dried corn with red and green peppers
- 1 can home-dried peas and carrots
- 1 can home-dried mushrooms (4½ ounces)

In the second plastic bag, mix together:

- 1 package tomato-flavored couscous (other flavors work also)
- 4 tablespoons dried egg
- 1 teaspoon dry onion
- ½ teaspoon garlic salt
- 1 teaspoon dried basil leaves, crushed

Carry separately:

- 1 teaspoon *Tabasco*® brand pepper sauce
- ½ cup shredded cheddar or Monterey Jack cheese

Preparation:

- Mix 2 cups water with the contents of the *first bag* in the Outback Oven pan.
- Set pan directly on the stove and bring to a boil.
- Reduce heat, cover and simmer 5-8 minutes or until the corn is tender.
- Remove from heat. Mix in ½ cup cold water and the contents of the *second bag*.
- Mix in pepper sauce. Spread cheese on top.
- Assemble the Oven and bake 10 minutes. Let stand 3 minutes.

Notes:

Dairyland Chicken Casserole

In the first plastic bag, mix together:

- 1 cup poultry chunk style TVP
- 1 tablespoon chicken-flavored bouillon
- 1 can home-dried carrots
- 1 can home-dried mushrooms (4½ ounces)
- 1 teaspoon dry onion
- ½ teaspoon garlic salt
- ¼ teaspoon celery salt
- 1/8 teaspoon black pepper

In the second plastic bag, mix together:

- 1 cup instant rice
- 2 envelopes cream of chicken dry *Cup-a-Soup*® mix

Carry separately:

- 1 teaspoon Worcestershire sauce

Preparation:

- Mix 3 cups water with the contents of the *first bag* in the Outback Oven pan.
- Set pan directly on the stove and bring to a boil.
- Reduce heat, cover and simmer 5-6 minutes.
- Stir in the contents of the *second bag* and Worcestershire sauce.
- Assemble the Oven and bake 10 minutes. Let stand 5 minutes.

Notes:

Ground Beef Pie

In the first plastic bag, mix together:
- 1½ cup ground beef style TVP
- 1 tablespoon instant beef-flavor bouillon

In the second plastic bag, mix together:
- 1 cup all-purpose baking mix
- 4 tablespoons dried egg
- ½ cup powdered milk

Carry separately:
- ½ cup shredded cheddar cheese
- 2 individual serving size packets of ketchup

Preparation:
- Mix 1¼ cup water with the contents of the *first bag* in the Outback Oven pan.
- Set pan directly on the stove and bring to a boil.
- Reduce heat and simmer 2-3 minutes.
- Remove from stove and stir in ketchup. Spread cheese on top and cover.
- Pour ½ cup water into the *second bag*. Mix by squeezing bag.
- Pour the batter over cheese in the Oven pan.
- Assemble the Oven and bake 10 minutes.

Notes:

Dried Chipped Beef with Biscuits

In the first plastic bag, mix together:

- 1 envelope country gravy mix (makes 2 cups)
- ¼ cup powdered milk
- 1 can home-dried mushrooms (4½ ounces)

In the second plastic bag, mix together:

- 1 package biscuit mix (8 ounces; 1¾ cups)
- 1 tablespoon powdered milk

Carry separately:

- 1 package dried beef (2¼ ounces)

Preparation:

- Mix 2¼ cups water with the contents of the *first bag* in the Outback Oven pan.
- Set pan directly on the stove and bring to a boil. Simmer until the gravy thickens.
- Remove from heat. Tear beef into small pieces and mix into the gravy.
- Pour ½ cup water in to the *second bag* and mix by squeezing the bag.
- Spread the batter over gravy in the Oven pan.
- Assemble the Oven and bake 10 minutes. Let stand 3 minutes.

Notes:

Hash and Beef Bake

In the first plastic bag, mix together:

- 1 cup ground beef style TVP
- 1 tablespoon instant beef-flavored bouillon
- 1 box dry hash brown potatoes (6 ounces)
- 1 can home-dried mushrooms (4½ ounces)
- 1 tablespoon dry onions
- 2 tablespoons dried egg
- 2 envelopes brown gravy mix (makes 2 cups total)

Preparation:

- Mix 3 cups water with the contents of the *first bag* in the Outback Oven pan.
- Set pan directly on the stove and bring to a boil.
- Stir well. Assemble Oven and bake 8 minutes. Let stand 3-5 minutes.

Notes:

Herb Omelet Bake

In the first plastic bag, mix together:

- ¾ cup dry egg
- ½ cup powdered milk
- ½ cup shredded mozzarella cheese
- ¼ cup all-purpose flour
- 1 teaspoon dried onion
- ½ teaspoon baking powder
- ½ teaspoon dried basil leaves, crushed
- ¼ teaspoon salt
- ¼ teaspoon pepper

Preparation:

- Mix 1 cup water with the contents of the *first bag* in the Outback Oven pan.
- Stir until ingredients are well blended.
- Assemble the Oven and bake 15 minutes. Let stand 5 minutes.

Notes:

Meat and Potato Pie

In the first plastic bag, mix together:
- 1 cup ground beef style TVP
- 2 tablespoons beef-flavored bouillon
- Potatoes (only) from a scalloped potatoes dinner
- 1 tablespoon dry onion
- ½ cup powdered milk
- ¼ teaspoon black pepper
- ½ teaspoon salt

In the second plastic bag, mix together:
- 1 package biscuit mix (8 ounces; 1¾ cups)
- 1 tablespoon dried egg
- 2 tablespoons powdered milk

Carry separately:
- 1 tablespoon Worcestershire sauce

Preparation:
- Mix 2½ cups water with contents of the *first bag* in the Outback Oven pan.
- Stir in Worcestershire sauce, bring to a boil, reduce heat, cover and simmer 5 minutes.
- Remove from heat and let stand 5 minutes. Don't skip this step.
- Pour ¾ cup water into the *second bag* and mix by squeezing the bag.
- Spread biscuit mix over the mixture in the Oven pan.
- Assemble the Oven and bake 12 minutes.

Notes:

Pasta-Chicken Vegetable Casserole

In the first plastic bag, mix together:
- 1 cup chunk chicken style TVP
- 1 tablespoon chicken-flavored bouillon
- 1 can home-dried peas and carrots
- Noodles (only) from a creamy pasta *Tuna Helper*® dinner mix
- ¼ cup powdered milk

In the second plastic bag, mix together:
- 1 envelope cream of chicken *Cup-a-Soup*® dry soup mix (2.4 ounces)
- Seasoning packet from the tuna mix

Carry separately:
- ½ cup French fried onions for topping (optional)

Preparation:
- Mix 3 cups water with the contents of the *first bag* in the Outback Oven pan.
- Set pan directly on stove and bring to a boil. Reduce heat and simmer 5 minutes.
- Add ½ cup cold water and the contents of the *second bag*. Stir well.
- Spread onions on top.
- Assemble the Oven and bake 12 minutes.

Notes:

Pasta Dried Beef Casserole

In the first plastic bag, mix together:

- 1 cup small macaroni
- 1 can home-dried peas and onions
- 1 tablespoon dry onion

In the second plastic bag, mix together:

- 1 envelope cheese broccoli dry soup mix
- ¼ cup powdered milk

Carry separately:

- 1 package dried beef (2¼ ounces)
- ¾ cup cornflakes, lightly crushed
- ½ cup shredded cheddar cheese

Preparation:

- Mix 2 cups water with the contents of the *first bag* in the Outback Oven pan.
- Set pan directly on the stove and bring to a boil. Reduce heat and simmer 5 minutes.
- Remove from heat. Add ½ cup cold water. Mix in the contents of the *second bag*.
- Tear beef into small pieces and stir into the mixture.
- Spread cornflakes and cheese on top.
- Assemble the Oven and bake 12 minutes. Let stand 5 minutes.

Notes:

Perfect Chicken and Pork Pie

In the first plastic bag, mix together:

- 1 cup poultry chunk style TVP
- 1 tablespoon chicken-flavored bouillon
- 1 can home-dried peas and onions
- ¼ teaspoon salt
- 1/8 teaspoon black pepper

In the second plastic bag, mix together:

- 1 envelope country gravy with sausage mix (makes 1 cup)
- 1 cup instant rice

Carry separately in a third plastic bag:

- 1 package biscuit mix (8 ounces; 1¾ cups)

Preparation:

- Mix 3 cups water with the contents of the *first bag* in the Outback Oven pan.
- Set the pan directly on the stove and bring to a boil. Simmer 2 minutes.
- Remove from heat and stir in the contents of the *second bag*. Mix well.
- Pour ½ cup water into the *third bag*. Mix by squeezing the bag.
- Spread over the top of the mixture in the Oven pan.
- Assemble the Oven and bake 12 minutes. Let stand 5 minutes.

Notes:

Pizza and Italian Cornbread Bake

In the first plastic bag, mix together:

- 1 cup ground beef style TVP
- 1 tablespoon beef-flavor bouillon
- 1 tablespoon dry onion
- 1 can home-dried mushrooms
- 1 envelope dry pizza sauce mix (1¼ ounces)

In the second plastic bag, mix together:

- 1 package cornbread muffin mix
- 1 tablespoon Italian seasoning
- 2 tablespoons dried egg

Carry separately:

- 1 can home-dried tomato paste (6 ounces)
- ½ cup grated mozzarella cheese

Preparation:

- Mix 1½ cups water with the contents of the *first bag* in the Outback Oven pan.
- Bring to a boil and stir in tomato paste. Remove from heat.
- Pour ¾ cup water into the *second bag* and mix by squeezing the bag.
- Spread over the mixture in the pan. Shake cheese on top.
- Assemble the Oven and bake 12 minutes.

Notes:

Railroad Bill's Pie

In the first plastic bag, mix together:
- 1 cup ground beef style TVP
- 1 tablespoon instant beef-flavor bouillon
- 1 tablespoon dry onion
- 1 package dry tomato soup mix (3½ ounces)
- 1 can home-dried corn
- ½ teaspoon chili powder
- 1 teaspoon salt
- ¼ teaspoon black pepper

In the second plastic bag, mix together:
- 1 package cornbread muffin mix (8 ounces; 1¾ cups)
- 1 tablespoon dried egg
- ¼ cup powdered milk

Preparation:
- Mix 2½ cups water with the contents of the *first bag* in the Outback Oven pan.
- Set pan directly on the stove and bring to a boil.
- Cover, reduce heat and simmer 5 minutes.
- Pour ½ cup water directly into the *second bag*.
- Mix by squeezing the bag. Add small amounts of water until well blended.
- Pour over the beef mix in the Oven pan.
- Assemble the Oven and bake 12 minutes. Let stand 5 minutes before serving.

Notes:

Sausage, Potato and Vegetable Bake

In the first plastic bag, mix together:

- 1 cup ground beef style TVP
- 1 tablespoon dry onion
- 1 can home-dried vegetables

In the second plastic bag, mix together:

- 1 box dried hash brown potatoes (6 ounces)
- 1 envelope country gravy with sausage mix (makes 2 cups)

Preparation:

- Mix 3 cups water with the contents of the *first bag* in the Outback Oven pan.
- Set pan directly on the stove and bring to a boil. Reduce heat and simmer 3-5 minutes stirring occasionally.
- Remove from the stove and mix in the contents of the *second bag*.
- Stir until well blended.
- Assemble the Oven and bake 10 minutes. Let stand 5 minutes before serving.

Notes:

Sloppy Joes and Cornbread

In the first plastic bag, mix together:

- 1 cup ground beef style TVP
- 1 tablespoon instant beef-flavored bouillon
- 1 tablespoon dry onion
- 1 can home-dried tomato paste (6 ounces)
- 1 can home-dried mushrooms (4½ ounces; optional)

In the second plastic bag, mix together:

- 1 package cornbread muffin mix (8 ounces; 1¾ cups)
- ¼ cup powdered milk
- 1 tablespoon dried egg

Carry separately:

- 1 envelope dry sloppy joe mix (1¼ ounces)
- ½ cup shredded cheddar cheese

Preparation:

- Mix 1½ cups water with the contents of the *first bag* in the Outback Oven pan.
- Bring to a boil and stir in sloppy joe mix. Remove from heat and cover.
- Pour ¾ cup water into the *second bag* and mix by squeezing the bag.
- Spread the cornbread over sloppy joe mix in the pan.
- Assemble the Oven and bake 10 minutes. Let stand 3 to 5 minutes.

Notes:

Tomato-Onion Burger Bake

In the first plastic bag, mix together:
- 1 cup ground beef style TVP
- 2 tablespoons instant beef-flavored bouillon
- 1 envelope dry onion or beefy-onion soup mix
- 1 tablespoon dry onion
- 1 tablespoon bacon bits (not the real meat kind)

In the second plastic bag, mix together:
- 1½ cups plain bread crumbs
- 2 tablespoons dried egg

In the third plastic bag, mix together:
- 1 package biscuit mix (8 ounces; 1¾ cups)
- 1 tablespoon dried egg
- 2 tablespoons powdered milk

Carry separately:
- ½ cup ketchup (6-8 individual serving size packages)

Preparation:
- Mix 1½ cup water with the contents of the *first bag* in the Outback Oven.
- Bring to a boil and simmer 2 minutes. Remove from heat.
- Stir in the contents of the *second bag* and ketchup. Mix well.
- Pour ¾ cup water into the *third bag* and mix by squeezing the bag.
- Spread over the mixture in the Oven pan.
- Assemble the Oven and bake 10 minutes. Let stand 3 minutes.

Notes:

Tortellini with Country Sausage Gravy

In the first plastic bag, mix together:

- 1 cup dry cheese-filled tortellini

In the second plastic bag, mix together:

- 1 package cornbread muffin mix (8 ounces; 1¾ cups)
- 1 tablespoon dried egg
- ¼ cup powdered milk

Carry separately:

- 1 envelope sausage country gravy mix (makes 2 cups)

Preparation:

- Mix 2½ cups water with the contents of the *first bag* in the Outback Oven pan.
- Bring to a boil, reduce heat, cover and simmer 10 minutes.
- Remove from heat and stir in gravy mix. Cover and let stand 5 minutes.
- Pour ¾ cup water into the *second bag* and mix by squeezing the bag.
- Pour over the tortellini in the Oven pan.
- Assemble the Oven and bake 10 minutes. Let stand 5 minutes.

Notes:

Turkey and Dressing

In the first plastic bag, mix together:

- 1 cup chicken chunk style TVP
- 1 can home-dried carrots
- Seasoning packet (only) from a cranberry-flavored dressing mix

In the second plastic bag, mix together:

- 1 package turkey gravy mix (0.9 ounce; makes 1 cup)
- Bread crumbs from the dressing mix

Preparation:

- Mix 3 cups water with the contents of the *first bag* in the Outback Oven pan.
- Set pan directly on the stove and bring to a boil.
- Reduce heat and simmer 5 minutes.
- Remove from heat and stir in ½ cup cold water.
- Stir in the contents of the *second bag* and mix well.
- Assemble the Oven and bake 10 minutes. Let stand 3 minutes.

Notes:

Turkey, Potato and Green Bean Casserole

In the first plastic bag, mix together:

- 1 cup chicken chunk style TVP
- 2 cans home-dried green beans
- 1 can home-dried mushrooms (4½ ounces)
- 1 teaspoon dry onion

In the second plastic bag, mix together:

- 1 box dry hash brown potatoes (6 ounces)
- 2 envelopes turkey gravy mix (0.9 ounce; makes 2 cups)

Carry separately:

- French fried onions for topping (optional)

Preparation:

- Mix 3 cups water with the contents of the *first bag* in the Outback Oven pan.
- Set pan directly on the stove. Bring to a boil, cover and simmer 5 minutes.
- Remove from heat and mix in the contents of the *second bag*.
- Assemble the Oven and bake 10 minutes.
- Let stand 3-5 minutes before serving. Spread French fried onions on top.

Notes:

Turkey Pot Pie

In the first plastic bag, mix together:

- 1 cup chicken chunk style TVP
- 1 can home-dried peas and carrots
- 1 can home-dried corn with red and green peppers
- 1 teaspoon dried egg

In the second plastic bag, mix together:

- 1 package biscuit mix (8 ounces; 1¾ cups)
- 1 tablespoon dried egg
- 1 tablespoon powdered milk
- 1 teaspoon dried sage

Carry separately:

- 1 envelope turkey gravy mix (0.9 ounce; makes 1 cup)

Preparation:

- Mix 2½ cups water with the contents of the *first bag* in the Outback Oven pan.
- Set pan directly on the stove and bring to a boil.
- Reduce heat and simmer 5 minutes or until the vegetables are tender.
- Remove from heat and stir in gravy mix. Blend well.
- Pour ½ cup water into the *second bag*. Mix by squeezing the bag.
- Pour biscuit batter over mixture in the Oven pan.
- Assemble the Oven and bake 10 minutes. Set stand 3 minutes.

Notes:

Worcestershire Hash

In the first plastic bag, mix together:

- 1 cup ground beef style TVP
- 1 tablespoon beef-flavored bouillon
- 1 package dry hash brown potatoes (6 ounces)
- 1 can home-dried vegetables
- ½ teaspoon chili powder

Carry separately:

- 1 tablespoon Worcestershire sauce
- ½ cup shredded Monterey Jack cheese

Preparation:

- Mix 2½ cups water with the contents of the *first bag* in the Outback Oven pan.
- Set pan directly on the stove and bring to a boil.
- Remove from heat and stir in Worcestershire Sauce. Spread cheese on top.
- Assemble the Oven and bake 10 minutes.

Notes:

Soups, Stews and Chowder Recipes

"Beautiful soup! Who cares for fish, game or any other dish? Who would not give all else for two pennyworth only of beautiful soup."

Lewis Carroll, *Alice in Wonderland*

"To make a good soup, the pot must only simmer or 'smile'."

French Proverb

Soups, stews, chowders are Wilderness Chef's staple meals. Fortunately they are also the easiest camp meals: Mix the dry ingredients at home, pour into a pan in camp, add water and let it simmer ('smile') for a few minutes. Make some dumplings to cook on top of the simmering broth and soup becomes a full meal.

Dumplings:

Dumplings are easy to make and add a lot to a soup meal. Add them to the top of the simmering soup about 5 minutes before it's ready to serve. To make dumplings, mix ¼ cup water with 1 cup all-purpose baking mix in a plastic bag. Squeeze the bag to blend the water and baking mix. Cut or tear a hole in the corner of the bag and squeeze out dollops of dough on top of the simmering stew. Cover and continue simmering for 5 minutes. The outside of the dumpling may be still moist, but the inside will be cooked. Test it with a knife by cutting a dumpling to see if the inside is done.

These are easy recipes to prepare under just about any conditions. However, there are a number of suggestions to consider when making these meals.

- Prepare soups in a large pan with a non-stick coating and a tightly-fitting lid to speed cooking and save fuel.

- Ingredients should be mixed with water and allowed to reconstitute for a half-hour or more before cooking.

- Bring them to a full rolling boil. Then cover the pan and reduce the heat to just simmer. Higher heat will not significantly reduce cooking time and just wastes fuel.

- Let soups stand for at least 5 minutes before everything is completely cooked. As long as the pan stays warm it will continue to cook.

- Don't add too much water. More can always be added, but it takes a long time and a lot of fuel to boil down a recipe with too much water.

- Soups can be eaten rolled in a flour tortilla or pocket bread by reducing the water by a cup or more to make a thick sauce.

- If a recipe uses pasta, select the smallest pasta possible such as angel hair or small shells. Smaller, thinner pastas cook faster.

- Choose different vegetables for variety. The kind and amount of vegetables will dramatically change the flavor and texture of the resulting dish.

- Don't skip the spices. The character of the flavor will change significantly by changing the spices.

- Make dumplings; they're easy to make and add a lot to a meal.

Varieties of soups are endless; create your own. Start with several packages of dry soup mix and enhance them with dried vegetables, pasta and a careful selection of seasonings and spices. Make it 'smile' and enjoy.

Anything Goes Potato Soup

In the first plastic bag, mix together:

- 1 package of dried potatoes (only) from a scalloped potatoes dinner mix
- 1 tablespoon dry onion
- 1 can home-dried peas and carrots
- 1 can home-dried green beans
- ½ teaspoon celery salt
- ½ teaspoon black pepper

In the second plastic bag, mix together:

- ¼ cup instant rice
- 1 can home-dried tomato paste (6 ounces)

Preparation:

- Mix 4 cups water with the contents of the *first bag* in the soup pan.
- Stir in tomato paste.
- Bring to a boil, reduce heat, cover and simmer 8 minutes.
- Stir in the contents of the *second bag*. Bring to a boil.
- Remove from heat, cover and let stand 5 minutes.

Notes:

Bacon and Bean Soup

In the first plastic bag, mix together:

- 3 tablespoons bacon bits (not the real meat kind)
- 1 can home-dried canned navy beans (15 ounces)
- 1 teaspoon celery salt
- 1 tablespoon dry onion
- ¾ teaspoon dried thyme, crushed
- ¼ teaspoon black pepper
- 1 bay leaf

Preparation:

- Mix 4 cups water with the contents of the *first bag* in the soup pan.
- Stir well until all lumps are gone.
- Bring to a boil, cover and simmer 5 minutes.
- Remove bay leaf before serving.

Notes:

Beef Noodle Soup

In the first plastic bag, mix together:

- 1 cup beef chunk style TVP
- 2 tablespoons instant beef-flavor bouillon
- 1 envelope beef and onion-flavored dry soup
- 1 can home-dried carrots
- ¼ teaspoon dried parsley
- ¼ teaspoon black pepper
- 1 cup small egg noodles or other small pasta

Preparation:

- Mix 4 cups water with the contents of the *first bag* in the soup pan.
- Bring to a boil and simmer 10 minutes.
- Cover and let stand 3-5 minutes before serving.

Notes:

Beef Soup

In the first plastic bag, mix together:
- 1 cup beef chunk style TVP
- 1 tablespoon instant beef-flavored bouillon
- 1 can home-dried peas and carrots
- 1 teaspoon dry onion
- ¼ teaspoon celery salt
- ¼ teaspoon garlic salt
- 1 teaspoon dried basil, crushed

Carry separately:
- 1 tablespoon Worcestershire sauce
- 1 can home-dried tomato paste (6 ounces)

Preparation:
- Mix 4 cups water with the contents of the *first bag* in a large pan.
- Stir well; mix in tomato paste and Worcestershire sauce.
- Bring to a boil, cover and simmer 5 minutes, stirring occasionally.

Notes:

Chicken and Salsa Soup

In the first plastic bag, mix together:
- 1 cup chicken chunk style TVP
- 1 can home-dried tomato paste (6 ounces)
- 1 can home-dried corn with red and green peppers
- 1 tablespoon instant chicken-flavored bouillon
- 1 teaspoon chili powder
- 1 package dry salsa mix (4 ounces)

Carry separately:
- 1 or 2 cups corn tortilla chips, broken
- ½ cup shredded Monterey Jack cheese (optional)

Preparation:
- Mix 4 cups water with the contents of the *first bag* in the soup pan.
- Stir until all dry ingredients have dissolved.
- Bring to a boil, cover and simmer 5 to 7 minutes or until the vegetables are soft.
- Serve by scattering corn chips and cheese on each serving.

Notes:

Chicken Couscous Stew

In the first plastic bag, mix together:
- 1 cup chicken chunk style TVP
- 1 tablespoon instant chicken-flavored bouillon
- 1 can home-dried carrots
- 1 teaspoon dry onion

In the second plastic bag, mix together:
- 1 package chicken-flavored couscous
- ¼ teaspoon garlic salt
- ½ cup raisins
- ¼ cup slivered almonds

Carry separately:
- 1 teaspoon *Tabasco*® pepper sauce

Preparation:
- Mix 4 cups water with the contents of the *first bag* in the soup pan.
- Bring to a boil, reduce heat, cover and simmer 5-6 minutes or until the carrots are tender. Mix in pepper sauce.
- Stir in the contents of the *second bag*. Bring to a full boil.
- Remove from heat, cover and let stand 5 minutes before serving.

Notes:

Chicken-Mushroom Ragout

In the first plastic bag, mix together:
- 1 cup chicken chunk style TVP
- 1 tablespoon instant chicken-flavored bouillon
- 1 can home-dried mushrooms (4½ ounces)
- 1 can home-dried carrots
- ½ teaspoon thyme, crushed
- ¼ teaspoon black pepper

Carry separately:
- 1 teaspoon horseradish mustard

Preparation:
- Mix four cups water with the contents of the *first bag* in the soup pan.
- Stir well until there are no more lumps.
- Blend in mustard.
- Bring to a boil, cover and simmer 5-8 minutes or until vegetables are soft.

Notes:

Chicken Noodle Soup

In the first plastic bag, mix together:
- 1 cup chicken chunk style TVP
- 1 tablespoon instant chicken-flavored bouillon
- 1 can home-dried peas and carrots
- 1 can home-dried corn or green beans
- ½ cup small noodles or other small pasta
- 1 teaspoon dry onion
- 1 teaspoons dried basil, crushed
- 1 teaspoon dried oregano, crushed
- ¼ teaspoon black pepper
- 1 bay leaf

Preparation:
- Mix 4 cups water with the contents of the *first bag* in the soup pan.
- Stir until there are no more lumps.
- Bring to a boil, cover and simmer 7-10 minutes or until vegetables are tender and pasta is cooked.
- Remove bay leaf before serving.

Notes:

Chicken Tortellini Soup

In the first plastic bag, mix together:
- 1 cup chicken chunk style TVP
- 1 tablespoon instant chicken-flavored bouillon
- 4 ounces dried cheese tortellini
- 1 teaspoon dry onion
- 2 cans home-dried vegetables
- ¼ teaspoon garlic powder
- ¼ teaspoon black pepper
- ½ teaspoon dried parsley
- ½ teaspoon thyme

Carry separately:
- ¼ cup grated Parmesan cheese (optional)

Preparation:
- Mix 4 cups water with the contents of the *first bag* in the soup pan.
- Bring to a boil, cover and simmer 12 minutes.
- Let stand 5 minutes. Don't skip this step.
- Stir well before serving and sprinkle Parmesan cheese on top.

Notes:

Chunky Potato Bacon Soup

In the first plastic bag, mix together:
- 1 package dry hash brown potatoes (6 ounces)
- ½ cup powdered milk
- 3 tablespoons bacon bits (not the real meat kind)
- 2 packages cream of chicken *Cup-a-Soup*® mix

Carry separately:
- 1 tablespoon Worcestershire sauce

Preparation:
- Mix four cups of water with the contents of the *first bag* in the soup pan.
- Mix in Worcestershire sauce and bring to a boil.
- Reduce heat and simmer 5 minutes, stirring frequently.
- Cover and let stand 3-5 minutes before serving.

Notes:

Corn and Crab Chowder

In the first plastic bag, mix together:
- Potatoes (only) from a scalloped potatoes mix
- 2 cans home-dried corn with red and green peppers
- ¼ teaspoon salt
- ¼ teaspoon dried thyme
- 1 teaspoon dry onion

In the second plastic bag, mix together:
- Sauce packet from the scalloped potatoes mix
- ½ cup powdered milk

Carry separately:
- 1 can crabmeat (6 ounces)

Preparation:
- Mix 3 cups water with the contents of the *first bag* in the soup pan.
- Bring to a boil, reduce heat, cover and simmer 8 to 10 minutes or until the potatoes are tender.
- Mix in the contents of the *second bag* and stir until well blended.
- Mix in crabmeat (undrained).
- Bring to a boil stirring constantly. Let stand 5 minutes before serving.

Notes:

Corn Chowder

In the first plastic bag, mix together:
- 2 tablespoons bacon bits (not the real meat kind)
- 2 cans home-dried corn with red and green peppers
- 4 teaspoons all-purpose flour
- ½ cup powdered milk
- ¼ cup powdered butter
- 1 tablespoon chicken-flavored instant bouillon
- 1 tablespoon dry onion
- ½ teaspoon celery salt
- ¼ teaspoon black pepper

In the second plastic bag, mix together:
- 1 cup instant rice
- 1 teaspoon parsley flakes

Preparation:
- Mix 4 cups water with the contents of the *first bag* in the soup pan.
- Bring to a boil, reduce heat and simmer 8 minutes or until corn is tender.
- Stir in the contents of the *second bag* and mix well.
- Remove from heat, cover and let stand 5 minutes. Stir well before serving.

Notes:

Cream of Chicken and Vegetable Soup

In the first plastic bag, mix together:
- 1 cup chicken chunk style TVP
- 1 tablespoon instant chicken-flavored bouillon
- 2 cans home-dried vegetables
- ½ cup powdered milk
- 1 tablespoon non-dairy coffee creamer
- 1 teaspoon dried basil, crushed
- ¼ teaspoon black pepper
- 1/8 teaspoon nutmeg

Preparation:
- Mix 4 cups water with the contents of the *first bag* in the soup pan.
- Bring to a boil, cover and simmer 5-7 minutes until the vegetables are soft.
- Stir well before serving.

Notes:

Cream of Chicken and Wild Rice Soup

In the first plastic bag, mix together:
- 1 cup chicken chunk style TVP
- 1 tablespoon instant chicken-flavored bouillon
- 1 package wild rice (4½ ounces)
- 1 can home-dried carrots
- ½ cup powdered milk
- 1 tablespoon non-dairy coffee creamer
- 1 teaspoon dry onion
- ½ teaspoon dried thyme

Preparation:
- Mix 4 cups water and the contents of the *first bag* in the soup pan.
- Bring to a boil, cover reduce heat and simmer 12 minutes.
- Remove from heat and let stand 5 minutes to thicken.

Notes:

Cream of Spinach and Pasta Chowder

In the first plastic bag, mix together:
- 1 cup small pasta such as small shells or angel hair
- 2 tablespoons bacon bits (not the real meat kind)
- 1 can home-dried corn with red and green peppers
- ¼ teaspoon garlic powder
- 1 teaspoon dry onion
- ½ teaspoon red pepper flakes

Carry separately:
- 2 packages of dry cream of spinach soup (3½ ounces)
- ¼ cup grated Parmesan Cheese

Preparation:
- Mix 3½ cups water with the contents of the *first bag* in the soup pan.
- Bring to a boil, reduce heat, cover and simmer 10 minutes.
- Remove from heat and mix in dry soup.
- Bring to a boil, reduce heat and simmer 5 minutes or until the pasta is tender.
- Add small amounts of water if it gets too thick.
- Sprinkle Parmesan cheese on top of each serving.

Notes:

Creamy Chicken and Vegetable Chowder

In the first plastic bag, mix together:
- 1 cup chunk poultry style TVP
- 1 tablespoon instant chicken-flavored bouillon
- 1 box potatoes and sauce from a scalloped potatoes dinner mix (5½ ounces)
- 2 envelopes cream of chicken *Cup-a-Soup*® dry soup mix
- 1 can home-dried corn with red and green peppers
- 1 can home-dried mushrooms (4½ ounces)
- 1 tablespoon dry onion

In the second plastic bag, mix together:
- ½ cup shredded cheddar cheese
- ½ cup crushed tortilla chips

Preparation:
- Mix 4 cups water with the contents of the *first bag* in the soup pan.
- Stir well until the lumps are gone.
- Bring to a boil, cover and simmer 10 minutes. Stir frequently.
- Remove from heat. Let stand 5 minutes to thicken.
- Shake the contents of the *second bag* on top just before serving.

Notes:

Ham and Bean Soup

In the first plastic bag, mix together:
- 1 cup chicken strip style TVP
- 3 tablespoons ham-flavored soup base mix
- 2 cans home-dried canned navy beans (15 ounces)
- ½ cup powdered milk
- 1 tablespoon dry onion
- 1 teaspoon celery salt
- ¼ teaspoon dried parsley
- ¼ teaspoon black pepper

Preparation:
- Mix 4 cups water with the contents of the *first bag* in the soup pan.
- Bring to a boil, cover and simmer 8-10 minutes or until the beans are tender.
- Stir well before serving.

Notes:

Hearty Chicken Stew

In the first plastic bag, mix together:
- 1 cup poultry chunk style TVP
- 1 teaspoon chicken-flavored bouillon
- 1 package potatoes (only) from a Julienne potatoes mix (4½ ounces)
- 1 can home-dried carrots
- 2 envelopes cream of chicken *Cup-a-Soup*® dry soup mix
- ¼ cup powdered milk
- 1/8 teaspoon black pepper

Preparation:
- Mix 3½ cups water with the contents of the *first bag* in the soup pan.
- Bring to a boil, reduce heat, cover and simmer 10 minutes. Stir frequently.
- Remove from heat and let stand 5 minutes.

Notes:

Hearty Split Pea Soup

In the first plastic bag, mix together:
- 3 tablespoons bacon bits (not the real meat kind)
- 1 tablespoon dry onion
- 1 can home-dried carrots
- ½ teaspoon salt
- ¼ teaspoon black pepper
- Pinch of dried marjoram

In the second plastic bag, mix together:
- 4 packages of instant split pea *Cup-a-Soup*® mix
- ½ cup instant rice

Preparation:
- Mix 4 cups water with the contents of the *first bag* in the soup pan.
- Bring to a boil, reduce heat and simmer 5 minutes or until the carrots are tender.
- Stir in the contents of the *second bag* and bring to a boil.
- Remove from heat, cover and let stand 5 minutes.

Notes:

Italian Chicken Bean Soup

In the first plastic bag, mix together:
- 1 cup poultry chunk style TVP
- 2 tablespoons instant chicken bouillon
- 1 can home-dried green beans
- 1 can home-dried tomato paste (6 ounces)
- ½ cup small pasta
- ½ teaspoon salt
- ¼ teaspoon garlic
- ¼ teaspoon dried oregano
- 1/8 teaspoon dill weed
- 1/8 teaspoon black pepper

Preparation:
- Mix 4 cups water with the contents of the *first bag* in the soup pan.
- Bring to a boil, reduce heat, cover and simmer 10 minutes or until pasta is tender.

Notes:

Manhattan Style Tuna Chowder

In the first plastic bag, mix together:
- 1 package potatoes (only) from a Julienne potatoes mix (4½ ounces)
- 1 can home-dried peas and carrots
- 1 can home-dried tomato paste (6 ounces)
- 2 tablespoons instant chicken-flavored bouillon
- ½ teaspoon black pepper
- ½ teaspoon garlic salt
- ½ teaspoon parsley flakes

Carry separately:
- 1 can tuna packed in water (6 ounces)
- ¼ cup grated Parmesan cheese

Preparation:
- Mix 3 cups water with the contents of the *first bag* in the soup pan.
- Bring to a boil, reduce heat, cover and simmer 10 minutes or until the potatoes are tender. Stir frequently.
- Mix in tuna (undrained) and stir well.
- Bring to a boil, remove from heat and let stand 5 minutes.
- Stir well and serve with a sprinkle of Parmesan cheese.

Notes:

Mashed Potato Soup

In the first plastic bag, mix together:
- 2 cups instant mashed potato flakes
- 1½ cups powdered milk
- 2 tablespoons chicken-flavored bouillon
- 2 teaspoons dry onion
- 2 teaspoons dry parsley
- 1½ teaspoons salt
- ¼ teaspoon white pepper
- ¼ teaspoon dried thyme
- 1/8 teaspoon ground turmeric

Preparation:
- Mix 4 cups water with the contents of the *first bag* in the soup pan.
- Bring to a boil and simmer 2-3 minutes. Let stand 5 minutes to thicken.
- To make a single serving, pour 1 cup boiling water over ½ cup of dry soup mix in small bowl. Stir until smooth.

Notes:

Pepperoni Pizza Pasta

In the first plastic bag, mix together:
- 1 cup small pasta such as shells or angel hair
- 1 can home-dried mushrooms (4½ ounces)
- 1 tablespoon dry onion

In the second plastic bag, mix together:
- 1 can home-dried tomato paste
- 1 package dry spaghetti sauce mix (1.5 ounces)

Carry separately:
- 1 sealed package of pepperoni slices (4 ounces)
- ½ cup grated mozzarella cheese

Preparation:
- Mix 3½ cups water with the contents of the *first bag* in the skillet or large pan.
- Bring to a boil, cover, reduce heat and simmer 8 minutes.
- Mix in the contents of the *second bag* and pepperoni slices.
- Bring to a boil and simmer until pasta is tender.
- Sprinkle mozzarella cheese over each serving.

Notes:

Pizza Soup with Pasta

In the first plastic bag, mix together:
- 2 envelopes tomato with basil soup
- ½ teaspoon garlic powder
- ½ teaspoon oregano leaves
- ¾ cup tiny pasta shells or orozo pasta

In the second plastic bag, mix together:
- ½ cup French fried onions
- ¼ cup grated mozzarella cheese

Preparation:
- Mix 3 cups water with the contents of the *first bag* in the soup pan. Stir well.
- Bring to a boil, reduce heat and simmer 8 minutes or until pasta is tender.
- From the *second bag*, sprinkle small amounts of French fried onions and cheese over each serving.

Notes:

Quick Beef and Vegetable Noodle Soup

In the first plastic bag, mix together:
- 1 cup ground beef style TVP
- 2 flavor packets from beef-flavored ramen noodles
- 2 cans home-dried vegetables
- 1 can home-dried tomato paste
- ¼ teaspoon black pepper
- ½ teaspoon chili powder
- ¼ teaspoon garlic powder

Carry separately:
- Noodles from 2 packages of ramen noodles, broken

Preparation:
- Mix 4 cups water with the contents of the *first bag* in the soup pan.
- Bring to a boil, reduce heat, cover and simmer 5 minutes.
- Stir in the contents of the *second bag*. Simmer 3 minutes.

Notes:

Ragin' Cajun Chicken Chowder

In the first plastic bag, mix together:
- 1 cup chicken chunk style TVP
- 1 teaspoon instant chicken-flavored bouillon
- 1 package *Rice-A-Roni* ® red beans and rice dinner mix (5 ounces)
- 1 can home-dried corn with red and green peppers
- 1 can home-dried tomato paste
- 1 tablespoon Cajun seasoning
- 1 teaspoon sugar
- ¼ teaspoon dried thyme, crushed

Preparation:
- Mix 4 cups of water with the contents of the *first bag* in the soup pan.
- Bring to a boil, cover and simmer 10-12 minutes or until beans are tender.
- Let stand 5 minutes before serving.

Notes:

Ravioli-Beef Tomato Stew

In the first plastic bag, mix together:
- 1 cup dry cheese-filled ravioli (4 ounces)
- 1 cup beef chunk style TVP
- 1 tablespoon instant beef-*flavored* bouillon
- 1 can home-dried green beans

In the second plastic bag, mix together:
- 1 envelope dry tomato-basil soup mix
- 1 tablespoon Italian seasoning mix (more or less to taste)

Preparation:
- Mix 4 cups water with the contents of the *first bag* in the soup pan.
- Bring to a boil, reduce heat, cover and simmer 12 minutes. Stir occasionally.
- Remove from heat, cover and let stand 5 minutes. Don't skip this step.
- Add the contents of the *second bag* and stir well.
- Bring to a boil and let stand 2-3 minutes before serving.

Notes:

Ravioli-Chicken Vegetable Stew

In the first plastic bag, mix together:
- 1 cup dry cheese-filled ravioli (4 ounces)
- 1 cup chicken chunk style TVP
- 1 tablespoon instant chicken-flavored bouillon
- 1 can home-dried peas and carrots
- 1 can home-dried corn

Carry separately:
- 2 envelopes chicken gravy mix (0.9 ounce each; makes 2 cups total)

Preparation:
- Mix 4 cups water with the contents of the *first bag* in the soup pan.
- Bring to a boil, reduce heat, cover and simmer 10 minutes.
- Remove from heat and let stand 5 minutes. Don't skip this step.
- Blend in chicken gravy mix and stir until the lumps are gone.
- Bring to a boil and let stand 3 minutes before serving.

Notes:

Spanish Rice Soup

In the first plastic bag, mix together:
- 1 cup ground beef style TVP
- 1 tablespoon beef-flavored bouillon
- 1 tablespoon dry onion
- 1 can home-dried green chili peppers (4 ounces)
- 1 can home-dried tomato paste (6 ounces)
- ½ teaspoon salt
- ½ teaspoon ground cumin
- 1 teaspoon pepper

Carry separately:
- ¾ cup instant rice
- 4 individual serving size packets of ketchup
- ¼ teaspoon *Tabasco*® pepper sauce

Preparation:
- Mix 4 cups water with the contents of the *first bag* in the soup pan.
- Bring to a boil, reduce heat, cover and simmer 5 minutes.
- Stir in ketchup and pepper sauce.
- Bring back to a boil, stir in rice and mix well.
- Remove from heat and let stand 5 minutes. Stir well before serving.

Notes:

Spicy Chicken and Vegetable Soup

In the first plastic bag, mix together:
- 1 cup chicken chunk style TVP
- 1 tablespoon instant chicken-flavored bouillon
- 1 can home-dried peas and carrots
- 1 can home-dried corn with red and green peppers
- 1 cup angel hair pasta broken into 2 inch pieces
- 1 teaspoon dry onion

Carry separately:
- 1 tablespoon *Tabasco*® pepper sauce (more or less to taste)

Preparation:
- Mix 4 cups water and the contents of the *first bag* in to the soup pan.
- Stir in pepper sauce.
- Bring to a boil, reduce heat and simmer 5 minutes until the pasta is tender.

Notes:

Super Quick Beef and Vegetable Soup

In the first plastic bag, mix together:
- 1 cup ground beef style TVP
- 1 tablespoon instant beef-flavored bouillon
- 2 cans home-dried vegetables
- 1 can home-dried tomato paste (6 ounces)
- 1 teaspoon chili powder
- ¼ teaspoon garlic salt
- ¼ teaspoon black pepper

Preparation:
- Mix 4 cups water with the contents of the *first bag* in the soup pan.
- Bring to a boil, cover and simmer 5-7 minutes or until vegetables are tender.
- Stir well before serving.

Notes:

Ten Minute Soup

In the first plastic bag, mix together:
- 1 cup strip steak style TVP
- 1 package dry potatoes from a scalloped potatoes dinner.
- 2 tablespoons beef-flavored bouillon
- 1 envelope dry onion soup mix
- 1 can home-dried tomato paste (6 ounces)
- 1 can home-dried peas and carrots

Preparation:
- Mix 4 cups water with the contents of the *first bag* in the soup pan.
- Bring to a boil, reduce heat, cover and simmer 12 minutes. Stir occasionally.
- Remove from heat and let stand 5 minutes.

Notes:

Tomato, Chicken and Mushroom Soup

In the first plastic bag, mix together:
- 1 cup poultry chunk style TVP
- 2 tablespoons chicken-flavored instant bouillon
- 1 can home-dried carrots
- 1 can home-dried mushrooms (4½ ounces)
- 1 can home-dried tomato paste (6 ounces)

Carry separately:
- ¾ cup instant rice
- 1 envelope dry Italian salad dressing mix

Preparation:
- Mix 4 cups water with the contents of the *first bag* in the soup pan.
- Bring to a boil, reduce heat, cover and simmer 5-8 minutes.
- Stir in Italian salad dressing mix.
- Mix in rice, remove from heat, cover and let stand 5 minutes.
- Stir well before serving.

Notes:

Turkey and Vegetable Stew

In the first plastic bag, mix together:
- 1 cup chicken chunk style TVP
- 2 cans home-dried vegetables
- ½ cup powdered milk
- 1 teaspoon dry onion
- 1 teaspoon dried basil, crushed
- ¼ teaspoon black pepper

Carry separately:
- 2 envelopes turkey gravy mix (0.9 ounce each; makes 2 cups)

Preparation:
- Mix 4 cups water with the contents of the *first bag* in the soup pan.
- Bring to a boil, cover and simmer 5 minutes until the vegetables are soft.
- Blend in gravy mix a little at a time while stirring continuously.
- Simmer 3-5 minutes stirring frequently.
- Cover and let stand 5 minutes to thicken. Stir well before serving.

Notes:

Pizzas, Pockets and Rollups

"The greatest dishes are very simple dishes."

Escoffier

In the case of wilderness dining, simpler is definitely better. Pizzas, pockets and rollups are what I call "hand-held meals." A hand-held meal is one that is to be eaten without benefit of plate or utensils. The recipes that follow are intended to be used as a topping for pizza crust or biscuits and as filling for rollups using flour tortillas or tucked inside pita bread pockets.

Hand-held meals result in far less clean up, faster meals and less fuel use since less hot water is needed to clean the pan. Also, nothing is more satisfying or filling than adding bread to an outdoor meal.

There are several things to consider while preparing these recipes:

- Stir frequently while cooking each recipe. The sauce will be thick and can burn easily.
- Have a cup of water on hand to add if the sauce gets too thick.
- When adding water, add only small amounts of about a tablespoon at a time.
- Just about any recipe can be made into a hand-held meal. Reduce the water by about a cup to start. Carefully watch how thick it gets and add water as needed as the meal cooks.

The recipes that follow can be eaten as a rollup, in the pocket of pita bread or as a pizza topping. They can also be spooned over rice, pasta, bagels or freshly baked breads from the Outback Oven.

Pizza Dough

This is the basic recipe and instructions for making pizza dough in the Outback Oven. Each recipe that follows in this section can be used as topping for the dough as well as stuffing for pita bread or filling for rollups.

In the first plastic bag, mix together:

- 1 package pizza dough mix (6½ ounces)

Preparation:

- Mix ½ cup water with the contents of the *first bag* in the Outback Oven pan.
- Stir with a fork until well blended.
- Spread the dough across the bottom of the pan with the back of a fork.
- Spread the topping of your choice over the dough.
- Assemble the Oven and bake 10 minutes at the high end of the "Bake" range.

Notes:

Barbecue Chicken

In the first plastic bag, mix together:
- 1½ cups chunk poultry style TVP
- 1 tablespoon instant chicken-flavored bouillon
- 1 teaspoon dry onion

Carry separately:
- 1 envelope *Shake and Bake*® barbecue chicken glaze (3½ ounces)

Preparation:
- Mix 1½ cups water with the contents of the *first bag* in a small pan.
- Bring to a boil and simmer 3-5 minutes.
- Mix in glaze and stir until well blended.
- Spread over pizza dough and bake, or serve in the pocket of pita bread or as a rollup.

Notes:

Cream of Chicken

In the first plastic bag, mix together:
- 1 cup chicken chunk style TVP
- 1 tablespoon chicken-flavored instant bouillon
- 1 can home-dried peas and carrots
- 1 teaspoon dry onion

In the second plastic bag, mix together:
- 2 envelopes cream of chicken-flavored of *Cup-a-Soup*®

Preparation:
- Mix 1½ cup water with the contents of the *first bag* in a medium pan.
- Bring to a boil, cover, reduce heat and simmer 7 minutes or until vegetables are tender.
- Stir in the contents of the *second bag* and mix until well blended.
- Spread over pizza dough and bake, or serve in the pocket of pita bread or as a rollup.

Notes:

Maple Chicken

In the first plastic bag, mix together:
- 1 cup chicken chunk style TVP
- 1 tablespoon chicken-flavored instant bouillon
- 1 can home-dried carrots

Carry separately:
- ¼ cup maple-flavored pancake syrup

Preparation:
- Mix 1 cup water with the contents of the *first bag* in a medium pan.
- Bring to a boil, cover, reduce heat and simmer 7 minutes.
- Stir in syrup and bring to a boil.
- Spread over pizza dough and bake, or serve in the pocket of pita bread or as a rollup.

Notes:

Sausage Gravy and Hash Brown Potatoes

In the first plastic bag, mix together:
- 1 package dry hash brown potatoes (6 ounces)
- 1 envelope country gravy with sausage (makes two cups)
- ½ teaspoon salt
- ¼ teaspoon pepper

Preparation:
- Mix 3½ cups water with the contents of the *first bag* in a medium pan.
- Bring to a boil, stirring constantly.
- Simmer for 2 minutes.
- Remove from heat, cover and let stand 10 minutes.
- Spread over pizza dough and bake, or in the pocket of pita bread or as a rollup.

Notes:

Sloppy Joes

In the first plastic bag, mix together:
- 1 cup ground beef style TVP
- 1 teaspoon beef-flavored bouillon
- 1 teaspoon dry onion

Carry separately:
- 1 can home-dried tomato paste (6 ounces)
- 1 envelope sloppy joe mix (1¼ ounces)

Preparation:
- Mix 1½ cups water with the contents of the *first bag* in a small pan.
- Bring to a boil and stir in tomato paste and sloppy joe mix.
- Bring to a boil and simmer 2-3 minutes stirring continuously.
- Spread over pizza dough and bake, or serve in the pocket of pita bread or as a rollup.

Notes:

Spicy Honey Chicken Chunks

In the first plastic bag, mix together:
- 1 cup chicken chunk style TVP
- 1 tablespoon chicken-flavored instant bouillon
- 1 can home-dried carrots
- 1 teaspoon chili powder
- ½ teaspoon ground mustard

Carry separately:
- ¼ cup honey
- 1 tablespoon soy sauce
- ½ teaspoon *Tabasco*® red pepper sauce

Preparation:
- Mix 1½ cup water with the contents of the *first bag* in a medium pan.
- Bring to a boil, cover, reduce heat and simmer 7 minutes or until vegetables are tender.
- Stir in honey, soy sauce and red pepper sauce and bring to a boil.
- Spread over pizza dough and bake, or serve in the pocket of pita bread or as a rollup.

Notes:

Sweet Beef Rollups

In the first plastic bag, mix together:
- 1 cup ground beef style TVP
- 1 tablespoon beef-flavor bouillon
- 1 teaspoon dry onion
- 1/8 teaspoon garlic powder
- Pinch of ground cloves

Carry separately:
- ½ cup orange marmalade

Preparation:
- Mix 1¼ cups water with the contents of the *first bag* in a medium pan.
- Bring to a boil and simmer 3-5 minutes.
- Mix in marmalade and stir until well blended.
- Bring to a boil.
- Spread over pizza dough and bake, or serve in the pocket of pita bread or as a rollup.

Notes:

Taco chips

In the first plastic bag, mix together:
- 1 cup ground beef style TVP
- 1 tablespoon beef-flavored bouillon
- 1 package taco seasoning mix (1.5 ounces)

Carry separately:
- 1 can home-dried tomato paste (6 ounces)
- 1 cup tortilla chips, somewhat crushed

Preparation:
- Mix 1¾ cup water with the contents of the *first bag* in a medium pan.
- Bring to a boil and simmer 3-4 minutes.
- Mix in tomato paste and stir until well blended.
- Sprinkle tortilla chips on each serving.
- Spread over pizza dough and bake, or serve in the pocket of pita bread or as a rollup.

Notes:

Turkey and Vegetables

In the first plastic bag, mix together:
* 1 cup chunk poultry style TVP
* 1 can home-dried peas and carrots

Carry separately:
* 1 envelope turkey gravy mix (0.9 ounce; makes 1 cup)

Preparation:
* Mix 2 cups water with the contents of the *first bag* in a small pan.
* Bring to a boil and simmer 5 minutes.
* Stir in turkey gravy mix and stir continuously until the lumps are gone.
* Spread over pizza dough and bake, or serve in the pocket of pita bread or as a rollup.

Notes:

One Skillet Meals

"In department stores, so much kitchen equipment is bought indiscriminately by people who just come for men's underwear."

Julia Child

Selecting the right cooking tool often determines the outcome of a meal. It's not necessary to use a skillet to prepare these meals even though I call them skillet meals. A pan from a cook kit will certainly work, but I prefer a skillet with a lid instead of a deeper pan, because it's easier to mix and stir the recipe with a spatula instead of a spoon, especially if it has a thick sauce. A spatula is also a much better tool to use to scrape the bottom of the pan to keep it from burning. Finally, I have found that a fry pan with a cover is a more versatile pan. On short trips, a fry pan with a lid is the only pan I carry. This is really the chef's choice and I recommend trying recipes both ways to determine a preference.

There are several things to consider when preparing these recipes:

- Whichever pan you choose, it should have a non-stick coating and a tightly fitting lid.
- Lightweight fry pans can be purchased from outdoor supply vendors. I have found an 8-inch pan works well.
- Remove the handle. It just adds weight and gets in the way in a pack. Use a much lighter pan gripper.
- Use a nylon spatula with a squared off end, not a rounded one. This way more surface area of the bottom of the pan can scraped at once and it's easier to get into the corners.
- Bring each recipe to a boil, stirring frequently. Then cover, reduce the heat and simmer.
- Let each dish stand covered for at least 5 minutes to finish cooking.

- To speed up cooking, soak dry ingredients for at least a half-hour before beginning to cook.

Skillet meals are the embodiment of one-pan camp cooking. Everything is prepared in a single pan; vegetables, meat, potatoes and sauce. All of the preparation is done at home and all the chef has to do is add water and heat. They are easy to prepare and can be easily modified to suit each chef's taste.

Alfredo Fettuccine Primavera

In the first plastic bag, mix together:
* 8 ounces fettuccine pasta
* 1 can home-dried peas and onions
* 1 can home-dried carrots
* 1 teaspoon dry onion
* ¼ cup home-dried or sun-dried tomatoes (optional)

Carry separately:
* 1 envelope dry Alfredo sauce mix (1¼ ounces)
* 2 tablespoons bacon bits (not the real meat kind)

Preparation:
* Mix 3 cups water with the contents of the *first bag* in the skillet or large pan.
* Bring to a boil, reduce heat, cover and simmer 10 minutes.
* Mix in dry Alfredo sauce and simmer 1-2 minutes. Let stand 5 minutes.

Notes:

Angel Hair Tuna Al Fresco

In the first plastic bag, mix together:
- 1 package angel hair pasta mix with seasonings
- 1 can home-dried peas
- ½ cup powdered milk
- 1 tablespoon dried onion
- ½ cup sun dried tomatoes (chopped)
- 1 tablespoon chopped almonds (optional)

Carry separately:
- 1 can tuna packed in water (6½ ounces)

Preparation:
- Mix 2½ cups water with the contents of the *first bag* in a skillet or large pan.
- Mix in tuna. Do not drain.
- Bring to a boil, reduce heat and simmer 5-7 minutes.
- Remove from heat, cover and let stand 5 minutes.
- Stir before serving.

Notes:

Beef and Vegetable Hash Browns

In the first plastic bag, mix together:
- 1 cup ground beef style TVP
- 1 tablespoon beef-flavored bouillon
- 1 package tomato soup
- 1 can home-dried mushrooms (4½ ounces)
- 1 can home-dried peas and carrots
- 1 can home-dried corn with red and green peppers

In the second plastic bag, mix together:
- 1 package dry hash brown potatoes (6 ounces)
- ¼ cup powdered milk

Carry separately:
- ½ cup shredded cheddar cheese

Preparation:
- Mix 4 cups water with the contents of the *first bag* in a skillet or large pan.
- Bring to a boil, cover, reduce heat and simmer 6-8 minutes.
- Stir in the contents of the *second bag* and bring to a boil.
- Cover and remove from heat. Let stand 5 minutes.
- Spread cheese on top of each serving.

Notes:

Bavarian Scalloped Potatoes

In the first plastic bag, mix together:
- Potatoes (only) from a scalloped potato mix
- 4 tablespoons bacon bits (not the real meat kind)

In the second plastic bag, mix together:
- Sauce mix from the scalloped potato mix
- ½ cup powdered milk
- 1 tablespoon sugar
- ½ teaspoon celery seed
- ¼ teaspoon black pepper

Carry separately:
- 1 tablespoon vinegar
- 1 tablespoon Worcestershire sauce
- ¾ cup sauerkraut, drained and packed into a food tube or wide-mouth bottle

Preparation:
- Mix 3¾ cups water with the contents of the *first bag* in a skillet or large pan.
- Bring to a boil.
- Reduce heat, cover and simmer 10 minutes.
- Stir in vinegar, Worcestershire sauce and sauerkraut.
- Blend in the contents of the *second bag*.
- Simmer 3-5 minutes or until the potatoes are tender.
- Let stand 5 minutes for the sauce to thicken before serving.

Notes:

Beef Italiano

In the first plastic bag, mix together:
* 1 cup ground beef style TVP
* 2 tablespoons beef-flavored instant bouillon
* 1 can home-dried green beans
* 1 can home-dried tomato paste (6 ounces)
* 1 tablespoon dry onion
* 1½ teaspoons salt
* 1 teaspoon basil leaves
* ½ teaspoon black pepper
* ½ teaspoon oregano leaves

Carry separately:
* 1½ cups instant rice

Preparation:
* Mix 4 cups water with the contents of the *first bag* in a skillet or large pan.
* Bring to a boil. Simmer 5-8 minutes or until the beans are tender.
* Stir in rice, remove from heat, cover and let stand 5 minutes.
* Stir well before serving.

Notes:

Beef Noodles and Gravy

In the first plastic bag, mix together:
- 1 cup ground beef style TVP
- 2 tablespoons instant beef-flavored bouillon
- 1 tablespoon dry onion
- 8 ounces small egg noodles (2 cups)

Carry separately:
- 2 envelopes brown gravy mix (7/8 ounce each; makes 2 cups)

Preparation:
- Mix 4 cups water with the contents of the *first bag* in a skillet or large pan
- Bring to a boil, reduce heat and simmer 8 minutes, stirring frequently.
- Stir in gravy mix and bring to a boil, stirring constantly.
- Let stand 5 minutes before serving.

Notes:

Beef, Pasta and Corn Skillet

In the first plastic bag, mix together:
- 1 cup ground beef style TVP
- 1 can home-dried corn
- 2 tablespoons beef-flavored bouillon
- 1 tablespoon dry onion
- 1/8 teaspoon black pepper
- 1 cup small pasta (4 ounces)

Carry separately:
- 1 can home-dried tomato paste (6 ounces)
- 1 envelope dry spaghetti sauce mix
- ¼ cup grated Parmesan cheese

Preparation:
- Mix 3 cups water with the contents of the *first bag* in a skillet or large pan.
- Bring to a boil, reduce heat, cover and simmer 8-10 minutes stirring occasionally.
- Stir in tomato paste and spaghetti sauce mix.
- Bring to a boil and simmer 3-4 minutes. Sprinkle Parmesan cheese on top.

Notes:

Beefy Spanish Rice and Vegetables

In the first plastic bag, mix together:
- 1 cup ground beef style TVP
- 1 tablespoon instant beef-flavor bouillon
- 1 can home-dried corn with red and green peppers
- 1 package Spanish rice dinner mix (7¾ ounces)
- 1 can home-dried tomato paste

Carry separately:
- ½ teaspoon *Tabasco*® pepper sauce

Preparation:
- Mix 3½ cups water with the contents of the *first bag* in a skillet or large pan.
- Stir in pepper sauce.
- Bring to a boil, reduce heat, cover and simmer 12 minutes or until rice is tender. Stir occasionally.
- Let stand 5 minutes before serving.

Notes:

Bow Tie Chicken Primavera

In the first plastic bag, mix together:
- 1 cup poultry chunk style TVP
- 1 teaspoon instant chicken-flavored bouillon
- 2 envelopes *Lipton*® Bow Tie Chicken Primavera pasta mix (4 ounces)
- 1 can home-dried peas and carrots
- 1 can home-dried mushrooms (4½ ounces)
- ½ cup powdered milk

Carry separately:
- ¼ cup grated Parmesan cheese for topping (optional)

Preparation:
- Mix 5 cups water with the contents of the *first bag* in a skillet or large pan.
- Bring to a boil, reduce heat, cover and simmer 10 minutes. Stir occasionally.
- Remove from heat and let stand 5 minutes. Don't skip this step.
- Stir well before serving and sprinkle cheese on each serving.

Notes:

Cantonese Beef

In the first plastic bag, mix together:
- 1 cup strip style beef TVP
- 1 tablespoon beef-flavored bouillon
- 2 cans home-dried Chinese vegetables (14 ounces each)
- 1 can home-dried mushrooms

In the second plastic bag, mix together:
- 1½ cups instant rice
- 1 teaspoon ground ginger
- 1 envelope mushroom gravy mix (¾ ounce; makes 1 cup)

Preparation:
- Mix 3½ cups water with the contents of the *first bag* in a skillet or large pan
- Bring to a boil, reduce heat, cover and simmer 8 minutes.
- Stir in the contents of the *second bag* and mix until well blended.
- Cover and let stand 5 minutes. Fluff with a fork before serving.

Notes:

Caramelized Potatoes and Vegetables

In the first plastic bag, mix together:
- 1 can home-dried peas and carrots
- 1 can home-dried corn with red and green peppers
- 1 can home-dried green beans
- Potatoes (only) from a scalloped potato mix

In the second plastic bag, mix together:
- 1 tablespoon dry onion
- ¼ cup brown sugar

Carry separately:
- ½ cup margarine

Preparation:
- Mix 2 cups water with the contents of the *first bag* in a skillet or large pan
- Bring to a boil and simmer 12 minutes.
- Remove from heat, cover and let stand 5 minutes.
- Stir in the contents of the *second bag* and margarine.
- Bring to a boil and stir until potatoes are well-coated. Serve immediately.

Notes:

Cheesy Vegetable Beef Dinner

In the first plastic bag, mix together:
- 1 cup chunk beef style TVP
- 1 tablespoon instant beef-flavored bouillon
- 1 package of potatoes (only) from a potatoes au gratin dinner mix
- 1 can home-dried peas and carrots or green beans
- 1 can home-dried corn
- 1 teaspoon dry onions

Carry separately:
- Sauce mix from the au gratin potatoes
- ¼ cup shredded sharp cheddar cheese (optional)
- ½ cup French fried onions (optional)

Preparation:
- Mix 3 cups water with contents of the *first bag* in a skillet or large pan.
- Bring to a boil, reduce heat, cover and simmer 12 minutes.
- Stir in sauce mix
- Simmer 2-3 minutes or until the potatoes are tender.
- Let stand 3-5 minutes before serving.
- Sprinkle cheese and French-fried onions on top of each serving.

Notes:

Chicken 'a la King

In the first plastic bag, mix together:
- 1 cup chunk poultry style TVP
- 1 can home-dried peas
- 1 can home-dried mushrooms (4½ ounces)
- ½ cup powdered milk
- ½ teaspoon salt
- 1/8 teaspoon black pepper

In the second plastic bag, mix together:
- 1 envelope chicken gravy mix (1 ounce)
- 1½ cups instant rice

Preparation:
- Mix 3½ cups water with the contents of the *first bag* in a skillet or large pan.
- Bring to a boil and simmer 5 minutes.
- Stir in the contents of the *second bag* and mix until well blended.
- Remove from heat, cover and let stand 5 minutes. Stir before serving.

Notes:

Chicken 'a la Parmesano

In the first plastic bag, mix together:
- 1 cup chicken chunk style TVP
- 1 tablespoon instant chicken-flavored bouillon
- ¼ cup powdered milk
- 1 can home-dried corn with red and green peppers
- 1 teaspoon dry onion
- 1¼ teaspoon dried basil

In the second plastic bag, mix together:
- Pasta and seasonings from a *Pasta Roni*® Parmesano dinner mix

Carry separately:
- ¼ cup grated Parmesan cheese (optional)

Preparation:
- Mix 3 cups water with the contents of the *first bag* in a skillet or large pan.
- Bring to a boil. Remove from the stove and stir in the contents of the *second bag*.
- Put pan back on the stove and bring to a boil, stirring constantly.
- Reduce heat, cover and simmer 5 minutes or until pasta is tender.
- Remove from heat and let stand 3 minutes. Stir well before serving.
- Sprinkle Parmesan cheese on each serving.

Notes:

Chicken with Rice, Apples and Cranberries

In the first plastic bag, mix together:
- 1 cup chicken chunk style TVP
- 1 teaspoon instant chicken-flavor bouillon
- 1 package chicken-flavored rice mix (6 ounces)
- 1 tablespoon brown sugar
- ¼ cup dried cranberries
- ½ cup dried apples, chopped
- ¼ cup raisins (optional)

Carry separately:
- ¼ cup slivered almonds (optional)

Preparation:
- Mix 4 cups water with the contents of the *first bag* in a skillet or large pan.
- Set pan directly on the stove and bring to a boil.
- Reduce heat, cover and simmer 12 minutes. Let stand 5 minutes before serving.
- Sprinkle almonds on top.

Notes:

Chicken with Rice, Apples and Cranberries (fast cooking)

In the first plastic bag, mix together:
- 1 cup chicken chunk style TVP
- 2 tablespoons instant chicken-flavor bouillon
- 1 tablespoon brown sugar
- ¼ cup dried cranberries
- ½ cup dried apples, chopped
- ¼ cup raisins (optional)

Carry separately:
- 1½ cups instant rice

Preparation:
- Mix 4½ cups water with the contents of the *first bag* in a skillet or large pan.
- Set pan directly on the stove and bring to a boil.
- Reduce heat, cover and simmer 3 minutes.
- Mix in rice. Stir well.
- Remove from heat, cover and let stand 5 minutes before serving.
- Stir before serving.

Notes:

Chicken Parmesan Pasta

In the first plastic bag, mix together:
- 1 cup poultry chunk style TVP
- 1 teaspoon instant chicken-flavored bouillon
- Pasta (only) from a *Betty Crocker*® Chicken Parmesan Pasta dinner (8 ounces)
- 1 can home-dried mushrooms (4½ ounces)
- 1 can home-dried green beans
- ½ teaspoon Italian seasonings

Carry separately:
- Sauce and topping mix from the dinner mix

Preparation:
- Mix 4½ cups water with the contents of the *first bag* in a skillet or large pan.
- Bring to a boil, reduce heat, cover and simmer 10 minutes.
- Add sauce mix and stir until well mixed with no lumps.
- Bring to a boil, remove from heat, cover and let stand 5 minutes.
- Sprinkle topping mix on each serving.

Notes:

Chicken with Pesto Pasta

In the first plastic bag, mix together:
- 1 cup chicken chunk style TVP
- 1 tablespoon instant chicken-flavored bouillon
- 1 can home-dried carrots
- 1 cup small egg noodles

Carry separately:
- 1 package dry pesto sauce mix (½ ounce)
- ¼ cup grated Parmesan cheese

Preparation:
- Mix 3 cups water with the contents of the *first bag* in a skillet or large pan.
- Bring to a boil, reduce heat, cover and simmer 7 to 8 minutes or until pasta is tender.
- Mix in dry pesto sauce and stir until well blended.
- Sprinkle Parmesan cheese over each serving.

Notes:

Chow Mein Skillet Dinner

In the first plastic bag, mix together:
- 1 cup ground beef style TVP
- 1 tablespoon beef-flavored bouillon
- 2 cans home-dried Chinese vegetables (14 ounces each)
- 1 teaspoon dry onion
- ½ teaspoon celery salt

In the second plastic bag, mix together:
- 2 envelopes of dry cream of chicken *Cup-a-Soup*®
- ½ cup instant rice
- 1 tablespoon brown sugar

Carry separately:
- 2 tablespoons soy sauce
- ½ cup chow mein noodles

Preparation:
- Mix 3 cups water with the contents of the *first bag* in a skillet or large pan.
- Bring to a boil, reduce heat, cover and simmer 5 minutes or until vegetables are tender.
- Stir in the contents of the *second bag* and bring to a boil, stirring constantly.
- Mix in soy sauce and remove from heat, cover and let stand 5 minutes.
- Serve with chow mein noodles on top.

Notes:

Chuckwagon BBQ Rice Roundup

In the first plastic bag, mix together:
- 1 cup ground beef style TVP
- 1 tablespoon instant beef-flavored bouillon
- 1 can home-dried corn with red and green peppers
- 1 package *Rice-A-Roni®* beef flavor dinner (rice and seasonings)

In the second plastic bag, mix together:
- 1 envelope sloppy joe sauce mix (1¼ ounces)
- 1 can home-dried tomato paste

Carry separately:
- ½ cup shredded cheddar cheese

Preparation:
- Mix 3 cups water with the contents of the *first bag* in a skillet or large pan.
- Bring to a boil, reduce heat, cover and simmer 5 minutes.
- Mix in the contents of the *second bag*. Stir until well blended.
- Bring to a boil and simmer 5 minutes.
- Remove from heat, sprinkle cheese on top, cover and let stand 5 minutes.

Notes:

Creole Green Beans

In the first plastic bag, mix together:
- 2 cans home-dried green beans
- 1 can home-dried corn with red and green peppers
- 1 tablespoon dry onion
- 4 tablespoons bacon bits (not the real meat kind)
- Several slices of home-dried or sun-dried tomatoes (optional)

In the second plastic bag, mix together:
- 2 tablespoons all-purpose flour
- 2 tablespoons brown sugar
- 1 teaspoon salt
- ½ teaspoon black pepper
- ½ teaspoon ground mustard

Carry separately:
- 1 tablespoon Worcestershire sauce

Preparation:
- Mix 2 cups water with the contents of the *first bag* in a skillet or large pan.
- Bring to a boil, reduce heat and simmer 5 minutes or until the corn is tender.
- Stir in Worcestershire sauce and the contents of the *second bag*.
- Mix until well blended. Heat gently until it begins to thicken.
- Remove from heat, cover and let stand 3 minutes before serving.

Notes:

Curried Beef and Rice

In the first plastic bag, mix together:
- 1 cup strip steak style TVP
- 2 tablespoons beef-flavored bouillon
- 1 tablespoon chicken-flavored bouillon
- ½ cup dried apple
- 1 tablespoon dry onion
- ¼ teaspoon curry powder (or more to taste)

In the second plastic bag, mix together (optional):
- 1 tablespoon parsley flakes
- 2 tablespoons chopped salted peanuts

Carry separately:
- 1½ cups instant rice.

Preparation:
- Mix 3 cups water with the contents of the *first bag* in a skillet or large pan.
- Bring to a boil, reduce heat, cover and simmer 8 minutes.
- Stir in rice and mix well. Remove from heat and let stand 5 minutes.
- Sprinkle with parsley and peanuts from *second bag* (optional).

Notes:

Dijon Chicken and Rice Skillet

In the first plastic bag, mix together:
- 1 cup chunk poultry style TVP
- 1 tablespoon instant chicken-flavored bouillon
- 1 package creamy chicken and mushroom-flavored rice mix (7 ounces)
- 1 can home-dried peas
- 1 can home-dried mushrooms (4½ ounces)
- ¼ teaspoon black pepper

Carry separately:
- 2 teaspoons Dijon-style mustard

Preparation:
- Mix 3 cups water with the contents of the *first bag* in a skillet or large pan.
- Stir in mustard. Bring to a boil, reduce heat and simmer 10 minutes.
- Let stand 5 minutes. Stir well before serving.

Notes:

Dried Beef Hash

In the first plastic bag, mix together:
- 2 tablespoons powdered milk
- 1 package butter buds
- 2 tablespoons dried onion
- 1 package brown gravy mix

In the second plastic bag, mix together:
- 3 cups instant mashed potatoes

Carry separately:
- 2 packages dried beef (2½ ounces each)

Preparation:
- Mix 3½ cups water with the contents of the *first bag* in a skillet or large pan.
- Tear dried beef into small pieces and stir in.
- Bring to a boil and simmer 1-2 minutes.
- Stir in the contents of the *second bag* and mix well.
- Remove from heat, cover and let stand 5 minutes.

Notes:

Easy Italian Rice Dinner

In the first plastic bag, mix together:
- 1 cup ground beef style TVP
- 1 tablespoon beef-flavored bouillon
- 1 can home-dried corn with red and green peppers
- 1 package Spanish rice mix (8 ounces)
- 1 tablespoon dry onion
- ½ teaspoon garlic powder
- 1 teaspoon dried oregano

Carry separately:
- Seasoning mix from the Spanish rice mix
- 1 can home-dried tomato paste (6 ounces)

Preparation:
- Mix 3½ cups water with the contents of the *first bag* in a skillet or large pan.
- Bring to a boil, reduce heat, cover and simmer 5 minutes.
- Remove from heat and let stand 5 minutes.
- Stir in the contents of the *second bag* and mix until well blended.
- Bring to a boil and simmer 5 minutes. Let stand 5 minutes.

Notes:

Easy Taco-Flavored Potatoes and Beef

In the first plastic bag, mix together:
- 1 cup ground beef style TVP
- 1 tablespoon beef-flavor bouillon
- 1 can home-dried corn with red and green peppers
- 1 envelope taco seasoning mix (1¼ ounces)

Carry separately:
- 1 package dry potatoes (only) from a scalloped potatoes dinner

Preparation:
- Mix 3¾ cups water with the potatoes in a skillet or large pan.
- Bring to a boil. Reduce heat, cover, and simmer 12 minutes.
- Stir in the contents of the *first bag*. Mix well and simmer 5 minutes.
- Remove from heat and let stand 5 minutes.

Notes:

Harvest Apple Chicken and Rice

In the first plastic bag, mix together:
- 1 cup poultry chunk style TVP
- 1 tablespoon chicken-flavored bouillon
- 1 package *Rice-A-Roni*® chicken-mushroom rice mix
- 1 can home-dried mushrooms (4½ ounces; optional)
- ½ cup dried apples, chopped
- ¼ cup dried cranberries or cherries

Carry separately:
- ¼ cup apple jelly

Preparation:
- Mix 2½ cups water with the contents of the *first bag* in a skillet or large pan.
- Bring to a boil and stir in apple jelly.
- Reduce heat, cover and simmer 10 minutes stirring occasionally.
- Remove from heat and let stand 5 minutes. Don't skip this step.

Notes:

Hearty Country Beef and Rice Dinner

In the first plastic bag, mix together:
- 1 cup ground beef style TVP
- 2 tablespoons beef-flavored bouillon
- 2 tablespoons bacon bits (not the real meat kind)
- 1 tablespoon dry onion
- 1 can home-dried corn with red and green peppers
- ¼ teaspoon black pepper
- ¼ teaspoon garlic

In the second plastic bag, mix together:
- 1½ cups instant rice
- 2 envelopes cream of broccoli dry soup mix

Preparation:
- Mix 3½ cups water with the contents of the *first bag* in a skillet or large pan.
- Bring to a boil and simmer 5 minutes or until the corn is tender.
- Mix in the contents of the *second bag* and bring to a boil.
- Remove from heat and let stand 5 minutes.

Notes:

Herbed Chicken and Rice

In the first plastic bag, mix together:
- 1 cup chicken chunk style TVP
- 1 tablespoon chicken-flavored bouillon
- 1 can home-dried carrots
- ¼ cup powdered milk
- 1 tablespoon dry onion
- ¼ teaspoon dried marjoram
- ¼ teaspoon dried thyme
- 1/8 teaspoon dried rosemary, crushed

Carry separately:
- 2 cups instant rice

Preparation:
- Mix 3½ cups water with the contents of the *first bag* in a skillet or large pan.
- Bring to a boil. Reduce heat and simmer 5 minutes or until the carrots are tender.
- Mix in rice and stir well.
- Remove from heat, cover and let stand 5 minutes. Stir before serving.

Notes:

Italian Mushroom Chicken

In the first plastic bag, mix together:
- 1 cup chicken chunk style TVP
- 1 tablespoon instant chicken-flavored bouillon
- 1 package mushroom gravy mix (¾ ounce)
- 1 envelope dry tomato with basil soup (3½ ounces)
- 1 cup small egg noodles
- 1 teaspoon Italian seasonings

Carry separately:
- ¼ cup grated Parmesan cheese

Preparation:
- Mix 3 cups water with the contents of the *first bag* in a skillet or large pan.
- Bring to a boil stirring frequently.
- Reduce heat, cover and simmer 8 minutes or until noodles are tender.
- Remove from heat and let stand 5 minutes.
- Shake Parmesan cheese on each serving.

Notes:

Lebanese Style Beef and Green Beans

In the first plastic bag, mix together:
* 1½ cups beef chunk style TVP
* 1 tablespoon instant beef-flavored bouillon
* 2 cans home-dried green beans
* 1 tablespoon dry onion
* 1 teaspoon garlic salt
* 1 teaspoon basil
* ½ teaspoon dry parsley
* ¼ teaspoon black pepper

Carry separately:
* 1 can home-dried tomato paste (6 ounces)
* 1 cup instant rice

Preparation:
* Mix 3 cups water with the contents of the *first bag* in a skillet or large pan.
* Bring to a boil, cover, reduce heat and simmer 8 minutes.
* Mix in tomato paste and stir until well blended.
* Bring back to a boil and simmer 2-3 minutes.
* Stir in rice, cover and let stand 5 minutes.

Notes:

Lemon Herb Chicken with Pasta and Vegetables

In the first plastic bag, mix together:
- 1 cup poultry chunk style TVP
- 1 tablespoon chicken-flavored bouillon
- 1 can home-dried green beans
- 1 can home-dried corn with red and green peppers
- 1 cup bow-tie pasta
- ¼ teaspoon black pepper

Carry separately:
- 1 envelope lemon-herb flavored chicken sauce mix (1 ounce)

Preparation:
- Mix 3 cups water with the contents of the *first bag* in a skillet or large pan.
- Bring to a boil, reduce heat and simmer 8 minutes.
- Stir in lemon-herb sauce and simmer 3-5 minutes.
- Remove from heat, cover and let stand 5 minutes.

Middle Eastern Style Beef

In the first plastic bag, mix together:
- 1 cup beef strip style TVP
- 2 tablespoons beef-flavored instant bouillon
- 1 tablespoon dry onion
- 1 can home-dried carrots
- ¼ teaspoon salt
- 1/8 teaspoon ground cinnamon

In the second plastic bag, mix together:
- 1½ cups instant rice
- ½ cup sliced or chopped almonds
- ¼ cup golden raisins

Carry separately:
- 1 tablespoon lemon juice

Preparation:
- Mix 3 cups water with the contents of the *first bag* in a skillet or large pan.
- Bring to a boil and simmer 5 minutes.
- Stir in lemon juice and the contents of the *second bag*.
- Remove from heat and let stand 5 minutes. Fluff with a fork before serving.

Notes:

Oriental Chicken with Ramen Noodles

In the first plastic bag mix together:
- 1 cup chicken chunk style TVP
- 1 tablespoon chicken-flavored bouillon
- 1 can home-dried oriental vegetables (12-15 ounces)
- 1 envelope teriyaki seasoning mix (¾ ounce)

Carry separately:
- 1 package Oriental flavored Ramen noodles

Preparation:
- Mix 2 cups water with the contents of the *first bag* in a skillet or large pan.
- Bring to a boil, cover and simmer 5-8 minutes or until vegetables are soft.
- Add the flavor packet from the Ramen noodles.
- Break noodles into small pieces and mix in with TVP and vegetables.
- Simmer 2-3 minutes stirring frequently.
- Serve alone or with chow mein noodles on top.

Notes:

Pasta Cheddar Burger Dinner

In the first plastic bag, mix together:
- 1 cup ground beef style TVP
- 1 tablespoon beef-flavored bouillon
- 2 packages cheddar cheese pasta and sauce mix (4½ ounces each)
- 1 can home-dried corn
- 1 teaspoon dried onion
- ¼ cup powdered milk

Preparation:
- Mix 3 cups water with the contents of the *first bag* in a skillet or large pan.
- Bring to a boil. Reduce heat, cover and simmer 10 minutes. Stir frequently.
- Remove from heat and let stand 5 minutes.

Notes:

Pasta-MexiCorn Scramble

In the first plastic bag, mix together:
- 1 cup small egg noodles
- 1 can home-dried corn with red and green peppers
- 1 teaspoon garlic salt
- ¼ teaspoon black pepper

In the second plastic bag, mix together:
- 1 package dried egg (6 ounces)
- ¼ cup grated Parmesan cheese
- ¼ cup powdered milk

Carry separately:
- 2 to 3 tablespoons of oil

Preparation:
- Mix 2 cups water with the contents of the *first bag* in a skillet or large pan.
- Bring to a boil, reduce heat, cover and simmer 8 minutes.
- Remove from heat and stir in ¾ cup cold water.
- Mix in the contents of the *second bag* and stir until well blended.
- Put pan back on the stove and scramble adding small amounts of oil if needed.

Notes:

Peaches and Chicken with Rice

In the first plastic bag, mix together:
- 1½ cup poultry chunk style TVP
- 2 tablespoons chicken-flavored bouillon
- 1 cup dried peaches, chopped

Carry separately:
- ½ cup apple jelly
- 1½ cups instant rice

Preparation:
- Mix 3½ cups water with the contents of the *first bag* in a skillet or large pan.
- Bring to a boil, reduce heat and simmer 8 minutes or until peaches are tender.
- Mix in apple jelly. Stir in rice and simmer until it starts to thicken.
- Remove from heat, cover and let stand 5 minutes.

Notes:

Polynesian Chicken

In the first plastic bag, mix together:
- 1 cup poultry chunk style TVP
- 1 tablespoon chicken-flavor instant bouillon
- 2 tablespoons brown sugar
- ½ teaspoon salt

In the second plastic bag, mix together:
- 1½ cups instant rice

Carry separately:
- ½ cup pineapple marmalade (orange will work)

Preparation:
- Mix 3½ cups water with the contents of the *first bag* in a skillet or large pan.
- Bring to a boil and simmer 3 minutes.
- Stir in marmalade and mix until well blended.
- Stir in the contents of the *second bag* and mix well.
- Remove from heat and let stand 5 minutes.

Notes:

Potatoes, Pasta and Vegetables in Broccoli-Cheese Sauce

In the first plastic bag, mix together:
- 1 package dry potatoes from a scalloped potatoes dinner mix
- 1 cup home-dried vegetables
- 1 cup small pasta
- 1 teaspoon dry dill weed
- ½ teaspoon dry parsley flakes

Carry separately:
- 1 envelope broccoli-cheese dry soup mix (3½ ounces)

Preparation:
- Mix 3 cups water with the contents of the *first bag* in a skillet or large pan.
- Bring to a boil, reduce heat, cover and simmer 12 minutes.
- Stir in soup mix. Simmer 2-3 minutes.
- Remover from heat, cover and let stand 5 minutes.

Notes:

Rancheros Skillet Dinner

In the first plastic bag, mix together:
- 1 cup ground beef style TVP
- 1 tablespoon instant beef-flavored bouillon
- Potatoes (only) from a package of au gratin potatoes mix (5¼ ounces)
- 1 tablespoon dry onion
- 1 can home-dried corn with red and green peppers
- 1 teaspoon taco seasoning

In the second plastic bag, mix together:
- Sauce mix from the au gratin potatoes
- ½ cup powdered milk

Carry separately:
- ½ teaspoon *Tabasco*® red pepper sauce (optional)

Preparation:
- Mix 3½ cups water with the contents of the *first bag* in a skillet or large pan.
- Bring to a boil, cover, reduce heat and simmer 12 minutes.
- Mix in the contents of the *second bag* and stir well.
- Simmer 5 minutes or until potatoes are tender.
- Add small amounts of water if the sauce gets too thick.
- Remove from heat and let stand 5 minutes before serving.

Notes:

Ramen Vegetable Beef Skillet

In the first plastic bag, mix together:
- 1 cup beef strip steak style TVP
- 2 tablespoons instant beef-flavored bouillon
- 2 cans home-dried Chinese vegetables (14 ounces)
- 1 can home-dried mushrooms (4½ ounces)
- ¼ teaspoon cayenne pepper

Carry separately:
- 2 tablespoons soy sauce
- 2 packages oriental flavor Ramen noodles

Preparation:
- Mix 3 cups water with the contents of the *first bag* in a skillet or large pan.
- Bring to a boil, reduce heat, cover and simmer 8 minutes.
- Stir in soy sauce and flavor packets from the Ramen noodles.
- Break noodles into pieces and mix in.
- Simmer 3-4 minutes or until noodles are tender. Stir frequently.

Notes:

Rotini and Chicken Dinner

In the first plastic bag, mix together:
- 1 cup poultry chunk style TVP
- 1 tablespoon chicken-flavor bouillon
- 1 package three-cheese rotini pasta and sauce mix (4½ ounces)
- 1 tablespoon dry onion
- ¼ cup home-dried tomatoes (optional)
- ½ cup powdered milk

Preparation:
- Mix 3 cups water with the contents of the *first bag* in a skillet or large pan.
- Bring to a boil. Reduce heat, cover and simmer 10 minutes.
- Stir frequently, especially after the sauce starts to thicken.
- Remove from heat and let stand 5 minutes.

Notes:

Scalloped Potatoes and Chicken

In the first plastic bag, mix together:
- 1 cup chicken chunk style TVP
- 1 tablespoon instant chicken-flavored bouillon
- 1 can home-dried peas
- Potatoes (only) from a scalloped potatoes dinner mix (8 ounces)
- ¼ cup powdered milk

In the second plastic bag, mix together:
- Seasoning package from the scalloped potatoes dinner mix
- ¼ teaspoon black pepper
- ½ teaspoon dry onion

Preparation:
- Mix 3 cups water with the contents of the *first bag* in a skillet or large pan.
- Bring to a boil.
- Remove from the stove and stir in the contents of the *second bag*. Mix well.
- Bring to a boil. Reduce heat, cover and simmer 12 minutes stirring occasionally.
- Let stand 5 minutes before serving.

Notes:

Skillet Beef and Hash Browns

In the first plastic bag, mix together:
- 2 cups ground beef style TVP
- 2 tablespoons instant beef-flavored bouillon
- 1 tablespoon dry onion

In the second plastic bag, mix together:
- 1 package dry hash brown potatoes (6 ounces)

Carry separately:
- ¼ cup ketchup
- 2 tablespoons Worcestershire sauce

Preparation:
- Mix 3½ cups water with the contents of the *first bag* in a skillet or large pan.
- Bring to a boil, reduce heat, cover and simmer 5 minutes.
- Mix in ketchup and Worcestershire sauce.
- Bring to a boil and mix in the contents of the *second bag*.
- Simmer 2 minutes. Remove from heat, cover and let stand 5 minutes.

Notes:

Southwestern Macaroni and Cheese

In the first plastic bag, mix together:
* 2 packages *Pasta-Roni*® shells and white cheddar cheese mix
* 1 can home-dried corn with red and green peppers
* 1 can home-dried chopped green chilies (optional)
* ¼ cup powdered milk
* 1 tablespoon chili powder (more or less to taste)

Preparation:
* Mix 3 cups water with the contents of the *first bag* in a skillet or large pan.
* Bring to a boil, reduce heat and simmer 8 minutes.
* Stir well, remove from heat and let stand 5 minutes.

Notes:

Spanish Rice and Chicken

In the first plastic bag, mix together:
- 1 cup chicken chunk style TVP
- 1 tablespoon chicken-flavored bouillon
- 1 can home-dried corn with red and green peppers
- Rice (only) from a package of Spanish rice mix (7¾ ounces)
- 1 tablespoon dry onion

In the second plastic bag, mix together:
- 1 can home-dried tomato paste (6 ounces)
- Seasoning mix from rice mix

Carry separately:
- Tortilla chips for topping

Preparation:
- Mix 3 cups water with the contents of the *first bag* in a skillet or large pan.
- Bring to a boil, reduce heat, cover and simmer 8 minutes or until rice is tender.
- Mix in the contents of the *second bag* and stir well.
- Bring to a boil and simmer 1-2 minutes.
- Remove from heat and let stand 5 minutes. Serve with tortilla chips on top.

Notes:

Spicy Onion Omelet Scramble

In the first plastic bag, mix together:
- 1 package dried hash brown potatoes (6 ounces)
- 1 package dried egg (6 ounces)
- ½ cup French fried onions

Carry separately:
- ¼ cup French fired onions
- 1 teaspoon *Tabasco*® pepper sauce (more or less to taste)

Preparation:
- Mix 2½ cups water with the contents of the *first bag* in a skillet or large pan.
- Bring to a boil, stirring constantly.
- Reduce heat, cover and simmer 5 minutes.
- Remove cover, and using a spatula turn the egg and potato mix over.
- Cover and cook another 5 minutes. Sprinkle French fried onions on top.

Notes:

Spinach Parmesan Linguine

In the first plastic bag, mix together:
- 8 ounces of linguine or angel hair pasta

In the second plastic bag, mix together:
- 2 envelopes cream of spinach dry soup (3½ ounces each)
- 1 tablespoon instant chicken-flavored bouillon
- ½ tablespoon garlic powder
- ½ cup powdered milk
- ¼ cup powdered buttermilk

Carry separately:
- ½ cup shredded Parmesan cheese (2 ounces)

Preparation:
- Mix 3 cups water with the contents of the *first bag* in a skillet or large pan.
- Bring to a boil, reduce heat and simmer 5 minutes.
- Mix in the contents of the *second bag* and stir until well blended.
- Simmer, stirring frequently for 5 minutes.
- Mix in Parmesan cheese and continue to heat until the cheese is melted.
- Serve immediately.

Notes:

Turkey and Rice with Vegetables

In the first plastic bag, mix together:
- 1 cup poultry chunk style TVP
- 1 can home-dried peas and carrots
- 1 can home-dried green beans
- 1 can home-dried mushrooms (4½ ounces)
- 1 tablespoon dry onion

In the second plastic bag, mix together:
- 2 envelopes dry turkey gravy mix (0.9 ounce each; makes 2 cups)
- 1 cup instant rice

Preparation:
- Mix 4 cups water with the contents of the *first bag* in a skillet or large pan.
- Bring to a boil, reduce heat, cover and simmer 8 minutes.
- Stir in the contents of the *second bag*.
- Bring to a boil. Cover, remove from heat and let stand 5 minutes.

Notes:

Tuna Tropicale

In the first plastic bag, mix together:
- 1 cup dried mixed tropical fruit (6-8 ounces)
- 1 tablespoon brown sugar
- ¼ cup sugar

In the second plastic bag, mix together:
- 1 cup instant rice
- 1 tablespoon corn starch

Carry separately:
- 1 can tuna packed in water (6 ounces)

Preparation:
- Mix 2 cups water with the contents of the *first bag* in a skillet or large pan.
- Bring to a boil, reduce heat, cover and simmer 6 to 8 minutes or until fruit is tender.
- Stir in tuna. Do not drain.
- Bring to a boil and stir in the contents of the *second bag*. Mix well.
- Remove from heat cover and let stand 3 minutes. Stir well before serving.

Notes:

Tuna with Creamy Asparagus Sauce

In the first plastic bag, mix together:
- 8 ounces spinach fettuccine pasta
- 1 can home-dried peas and carrots

Carry separately:
- 1 can tuna packed in water (6 ounces)
- 2 envelopes cream of asparagus dry soup (3½ ounces)

Preparation:
- Mix 2½ cups water with the contents of the *first bag* in a skillet or large pan.
- Bring to a boil, reduce heat, cover and simmer 5 minutes.
- Remove from heat and let stand 5 minutes.
- Stir in tuna (undrained) and soup mix.
- Bring to a boil, remove from heat and let stand 3 minutes.

Notes:

Vegetable Beef Dinner

In the first plastic bag, mix together:
- 1 cup chunk beef style TVP
- 1 tablespoon instant beef-flavored bouillon
- 1 package of potatoes (only) from a scalloped potato dinner mix
- 1 can home-dried peas and carrots
- 1 can home-dried corn
- 1 teaspoon dry onions

Carry separately:
- 1 packet brown gravy mix (7/8 ounce)
- ½ teaspoon *Tabasco*® pepper sauce (optional)

Preparation:
- Mix 3 cups water with contents of the *first bag* in a skillet or large pan.
- Bring to a boil, reduce heat, cover and simmer 10 minutes.
- Mix in brown gravy pepper sauce. Stir until well blended.
- Simmer 2-3 minutes or until potatoes are tender. Let stand 5 minutes.

Notes:

Western Macaroni Dinner

In the first plastic bag, mix together:
- 1 cup ground beef style TVP
- 2 tablespoons beef-flavored bouillon
- 1 cup elbow macaroni
- 2 cans home-dried corn with red and green peppers
- 1 tablespoon dry onion
- ½ teaspoon celery salt
- 1/8 teaspoon black pepper

Carry separately:
- 1 can home-dried tomato paste (6 ounces)
- 1 tablespoon Worcestershire sauce

Preparation:
- Mix 3 cups water with the contents of the *first bag* in a skillet or large pan.
- Stir in tomato paste and Worcestershire sauce. Mix until well blended.
- Bring to a boil, reduce heat and simmer 10 minutes, stirring occasionally.

Notes:

Zesty Chicken and Rice

In the first plastic bag, mix together:
- 1 cup poultry chunk style TVP
- 2 tablespoons chicken-flavored bouillon
- 1 envelope tomato or tomato with basil dry soup mix
- 1 can home-dried peas
- 1 teaspoon dried basil leaves
- ¼ teaspoon garlic powder

Carry separately:
- ½ teaspoon *Tabasco*® pepper sauce
- 1 cup instant rice

Preparation:
- Mix 3½ cups water with the contents of the *first bag* in a skillet or large pan.
- Bring to a boil, reduce heat, cover and simmer 7 minutes. Stir frequently.
- Stir in pepper sauce and rice. Mix until well blended.
- Remove from heat, cover and let stand 5 minutes.

Notes:

Dessert Recipes

"People come to me with their heads held high and announce that they do not eat sugar anymore, as though they have tackled one of life's deadly sins. My response is to ask them how long they have had this problem and if they have considered seeing a psychiatrist."
Emily Lunchitte, American pastry chef and cookbook author

I have a penchant for cooked, warm desserts even when the weather is hot. The recipes in this section certainly reflect this. Also, I prefer to have dinner and wait a few hours before preparing dessert, sometimes until it begins to get dark. In this way, dessert becomes a unifying evening social event as well as satisfying appetites. Over the years I have had great success converting people to this philosophy although some insist on having dessert right after the meal and then again in the evening. After tallying up the meals, I discovered that on most trips, I prepare more desserts than dinners; sometimes two or three times as many[*].

However the group chooses to do it, never skip dessert. A friend of mine told me that her grandmother's reason to eat dessert was to "lock up your stomach with something sweet." Words of wisdom after a hard day. Make desserts the centerpiece of evening activities.

---

[*] Sometimes after a particularly hard day, it's impossible to not keep making desserts one after the other as long as the crowd demands them: a chef's ultimate accolade.

Almond-Oatmeal Cake

In the first plastic bag, mix together:
- 1 package *Jiffy*® white or yellow cake mix (9 ounces, 1½ cups)
- ½ cup quick-cooking oats
- 2 tablespoons dried egg

Carry separately:
- 1 tablespoon almond extract
- ½ cup powdered sugar for topping

Preparation:
- Mix ½ cup water with the contents of the *first bag* in the Outback Oven.
- Stir until well blended. Mix in almond extract.
- Assemble the Oven and bake 10 minutes.
- Let stand 5 minutes before serving. Shake powdered sugar on top.

Notes:

Apple Cake Country Style

In the first plastic bag, mix together:
- 1 cup dried apples, chopped
- ¼ cup raisins

In the second plastic bag, mix together:
- 1 package nut bread (8 ounces; 1¾ cups)
- ¼ cup sugar
- ¼ cup walnuts, chopped
- 2 tablespoons dried egg
- 1 teaspoon ground cinnamon
- ¼ teaspoon nutmeg

Preparation:
- Mix 1 cup water with the contents of the *first bag* in the Outback Oven pan.
- Set pan directly on the stove and bring to a boil.
- Reduce heat, cover and simmer 5 minutes.
- Remove from heat and let stand 5 minutes.
- Add ½ cup cold water and the contents of the *second bag*. Stir until well blended.
- Assemble the Oven and bake 12 minutes.

Notes:

Apple Pie Brownie Cake

In the first plastic bag, mix together:
- 1 cup dried apples, chopped
- ½ cup white sugar
- 2 tablespoons brown sugar
- 1 teaspoon ground cinnamon

In the second plastic bag, mix together:
- 1 package *Jiffy*® brownie mix (8 ounces; 1½ cups)
- 3 tablespoons dried egg

Carry separately:
- 1 tablespoon vanilla extract
- 1 tablespoon cornstarch

Preparation:
- Mix ¾ cup water with the contents of the *first bag* in the Outback Oven pan.
- Set the pan directly on the stove and bring to a boil.
- Reduce head and simmer 1-2 minutes. Stir in cornstarch and mix well.
- Remove from heat, cover and let stand 5 minutes.
- Pour ½ cup water and the vanilla into the *second bag*. Mix by squeezing the bag.
- Pour evenly over the apples.
- Assemble the Oven and bake 10 minutes. Let stand 5 minutes.

Notes:

Banana Oat Bread Pudding

In the first plastic bag, mix together:
- 4 slices bread (fresh or several days old), torn into small pieces
- 1 cup quick cooking oats
- ¾ cup powdered milk

In the second plastic bag, mix together:
- 2 very ripe bananas, sliced
- ¼ cup brown sugar
- ½ cup raisins

Preparation:
- Mix 1¾ cups water with the contents of the *first bag* in the Outback Oven pan.
- Cover and let stand 10 minutes.
- Stir in the contents of the *second bag*. Mix with a fork until well blended.
- Assemble the Oven and bake 12 minutes. Let stand 10 minutes before serving.

Notes:

Bonanza Brownies

In the first plastic bag, mix together:
- 1 package *Jiffy*® brownie mix (8 ounces; 1½ cups)
- 2 tablespoons dried egg
- ¼ cup powdered milk

Carry separately:
- 1 cup granola cereal with fruit and nuts

Preparation:
- Mix ½ cup water with the contents of the *first bag* in the Outback Oven pan.
- Stir in granola cereal.
- Assemble the Oven and bake 8 minutes. Let stand 5 minutes.

Notes:

Butter-Pecan Shortbread

In the first plastic bag, mix together:
- 1¼ cups all-purpose flour
- ¼ cup brown sugar, packed
- ¼ cup chopped pecans

Carry separately:
- ½ teaspoon vanilla extract
- ½ teaspoon almond extract
- ½ cup margarine

Preparation:
- Mix ½ cup water with the contents of the *first bag* in the Outback Oven pan.
- Stir in extracts and margarine. Mix well until crumbly.
- Add water one teaspoon at a time until the batter can be just spread.
- Assemble the Oven and bake 10 minutes. Let stand 5 minutes.

Notes:

Cherry Scones

In the first plastic bag, mix together:
- 1¾ cups all-purpose flour
- ¼ cup sugar
- 1½ teaspoons cream of tartar
- ¾ teaspoon baking soda
- ¼ teaspoon salt
- 2 tablespoons powdered buttermilk
- 1 tablespoon non-dairy coffee creamer
- ½ cup dried cherries

Carry separately:
- 1 teaspoon lemon juice
- 3 tablespoons sugar

Preparation:
- Mix ½ cup water with the contents of the *first bag* in the Outback Oven pan.
- Stir well and add lemon juice.
- Add water 1 tablespoon at a time until the batter can be just spread.
- Spread evenly in Oven and score with a knife to make 6-8 separate scones.
- Sprinkle sugar on each scone. Assemble the Oven and bake 12 minutes.
- Let stand 5 minutes.

Notes:

Chocolate Chip Coffee Cake

In the first plastic bag, mix together:
- 1½ cups all-purpose flour
- ¾ cup sugar
- 2 tablespoons dry egg
- ¼ cup powdered milk
- ¼ cup semisweet chocolate chips
- 1 teaspoon baking powder
- ½ teaspoon baking soda
- 1 teaspoon ground cinnamon
- ¼ teaspoon salt

Carry separately:
- 1 teaspoon vanilla extract
- ¼ cup chopped nuts

Preparation:
- Mix ¾ cup water with the contents of the *first bag* in the Outback Oven pan.
- Stir in vanilla and mix until the batter is smooth. Spread nuts on top.
- Assemble the Oven and bake 12 minutes. Let stand 5 minutes.

Notes:

Chocolate Chip Shortbread

In the first plastic bag, mix together:
- 1 cup all-purpose flour
- ¾ cup powdered sugar
- ½ cup semi-sweet chocolate chips
- 3 tablespoons corn starch
- 1/8 teaspoon salt

Carry separately:
- ½ teaspoon almond extract
- ½ teaspoon vanilla extract

Preparation:
- Mix ½ cup water with the contents of the *first bag* in the Outback Oven pan.
- Stir in almond and vanilla extract and mix well.
- Assemble the Oven and bake 10 minutes. Let stand 5 minutes.

Notes:

Chocolate-Coconut Rice Squares

In the first plastic bag, mix together:
- 1½ cups instant rice
- ½ cup semi-sweet chocolate chips
- ¼ cup coconut
- ¼ cup sugar
- ½ teaspoon salt

Preparation:
- Mix 1½ cups water with the contents of the *first bag* in a medium pan.
- Bring to a full boil stirring constantly.
- Remove from heat and let stand to cool about 20 minutes.
- Cut into squares to serve.

Notes:

Chocolate Crunchers

In the first plastic bag, mix together:
- 1¾ cups German chocolate cake mix
- 2 tablespoons dried egg
- ½ cup rice cereal, lightly crushed
- ½ cup quick cooking oats
- ¼ cup plain M&Ms®
- 1 tablespoon chopped nuts (optional)

Carry separately:
- ¼ cup powdered sugar for topping (optional)

Preparation:
- Mix ¾ cup water with the contents of the *first bag* in the Outback Oven pan.
- Stir until well blended. Spread evenly over the bottom of the pan.
- Assemble the Oven and bake 12 minutes. Let stand 5 minutes.
- Dust sugar over the top.

Notes:

Chocolate Peanut Butter Coconut Bars

In the first plastic bag, mix together:
* 1 package *Jiffy*® fudge frosting mix (7½ ounces; 1½ cups)
* ¼ cup flour
* 1 tablespoon dried egg
* ½ cup coconut
* ½ cup chopped nuts

Carry separately:
* ½ cup crunchy peanut butter

Preparation:
* Mix ½ cup water with the contents of the *first bag* in the Outback Oven pan.
* Stir in peanut butter and blend well.
* Add water one teaspoon at a time until the batter is smooth.
* Assemble the Oven and bake 10 minutes. Let stand 5 minutes.

Notes:

Chunky Apple-Walnut Coffee Cake

In the first plastic bag, mix together:
- 1¾ cups all-purpose baking mix
- 1 tablespoon dried egg
- ¼ cup brown sugar, packed
- ¼ cup walnuts, chopped
- ¼ cup powdered milk
- ½ teaspoon ground cinnamon

Carry separately:
- ½ cup dried apples, chopped

Preparation:
- Mix ¾ cup water with the apples in the Outback Oven pan.
- Set pan directly on the stove and bring to a boil.
- Reduce heat, cover and simmer 5 minutes.
- Remove from heat and stir in the contents of the *first bag*.
- Stir well and spread batter over the bottom of the pan.
- Assemble the Oven and bake 12 minutes. Let stand 5 minutes.

Notes:

Cranberry-Apple Porridge

In the first plastic bag, mix together:
* ½ cup dried apples, chopped
* ½ cup dried cranberries or cherries

In the second plastic bag, mix together:
* 1 cup quick cooking oats
* ½ cup powdered milk
* ¼ cup packed brown sugar
* ¼ teaspoon ground cinnamon
* Pinch of salt

Preparation:
* Mix 2 cups water with the contents of the *first bag* in a medium pan.
* Bring to a boil and simmer 5 minutes or until the apples are soft.
* Stir in the contents of the *second bag*.
* Bring to a boil and cook 1 minute, stirring constantly.
* Remove from heat and let stand 3 minutes.

Notes:

Dates 'n Apples 'n Nuts Porridge

In the first plastic bag, mix together:
- ¼ cup dates, chopped
- ½ cup granola cereal with fruit and nuts
- ¼ cup quick cooking oats
- ¼ cup dried apples
- 1 tablespoon walnuts, chopped
- 2 tablespoons brown sugar
- ¼ teaspoon ground cinnamon

Carry separately:
- ¼ pancake syrup (optional)

Preparation:
- Mix 1 cup water with the contents of the *first bag* in a medium pan.
- Bring to a boil, reduce heat, cover and simmer 5 minutes.
- Remove from heat and let stand 5 minutes.
- Drizzle a little pancake syrup on each serving.

Notes:

Easy Scratch Cake

In the first plastic bag, mix together:
- 1½ cups all-purpose baking mix
- ¾ cup sugar
- 2 tablespoons dried egg
- ¼ cup powdered milk

Carry separately:
- 1 teaspoon vanilla
- ½ cup powdered sugar for topping or glaze

Preparation:
- Mix ¾ cup water with the contents of the *first bag* in the Outback Oven pan.
- Stir in vanilla. Mix until well blended.
- Assemble the Oven and bake 10 minutes. Let stand 5 minutes.
- Sprinkle sugar on top. Make glaze by mixing 2 teaspoons of water with sugar.

Notes:

Fruit and Oatmeal Crisp

In the first plastic bag, mix together:
- ¾ cup dry fruit, chopped
- ¼ cup sugar

In the second plastic bag, mix together:
- ½ cup pancake mix
- ½ cup quick cooking oats
- ¼ cup brown sugar, packed
- ¼ teaspoon ground cinnamon

Preparation:
- Mix 1 cup water with the contents of the *first bag* in the Outback Oven pan.
- Set pan directly on the stove and bring to a boil.
- Reduce heat, cover and simmer 5 minutes.
- Remove from heat and let stand 5 minutes.
- Shake the *second bag* and spread over fruit in the pan.
- Assemble the Oven and bake 10 minutes. Let stand 5 minutes.

Notes:

Fruit Salsa and Pancake Bake

In the first plastic bag, mix together:
- 1 package mixed dried fruit, chopped (6 ounces)
- 2 tablespoons sugar
- 1 tablespoon brown sugar

In the second plastic bag, mix together:
- 1 cup complete (just add water) pancake mix

Carry separately:
- 3 tablespoons any flavor preserves (don't use jelly)

Preparation:
- Mix ¾ cup water with the contents of the *first bag* in the Outback Oven pan.
- Set pan directly on stove and bring to a boil. Reduce heat, cover and simmer 5 minutes.
- Remove from heat, stir in preserves, cover and let stand 5 minutes.
- Pour ½ cup water into the *second bag*. Mix by squeezing the bag.
- Spread the batter over the fruit in the Oven pan.
- Assemble the Oven and bake 8 minutes.

Notes:

Fudge Pecan Tart

In the first plastic bag, mix together:
- ¾ cup brown sugar, packed
- 3 tablespoons unsweetened cocoa (not hot chocolate)
- 2 tablespoons dried egg
- ½ cup chopped pecans
- ½ cup chocolate chips

In the second plastic bag, mix together:
- 1 package *Jiffy*® white or yellow cake mix (9 ounces; 1½ cups)
- 1 tablespoon dried egg

Carry separately:
- 1 teaspoon vanilla extract

Preparation:
- Mix ¼ cup water with the contents of the *first bag* in the Outback Oven pan.
- Add vanilla and stir until well blended. Spread over the bottom of the Oven pan.
- Pour ½ cup water into the *second bag*. Mix by squeezing the bag.
- Spread batter over mixture in the Oven pan.
- Assemble the Oven and bake 10 minutes. Let stand 5 minutes.

Notes:

Macaroon Brownies

In the first plastic bag, mix together:
- 1 package *Jiffy*® brownie mix (9 ounces; 1½ cups)
- 2 tablespoons dried egg
- ¼ cup plain *M&Ms*® or similar candy
- 1 cup coconut

Preparation:
- Mix ½ cup water with the contents of the *first bag* in the Outback Oven pan.
- Stir until well blended. Spread evenly over the bottom of the pan.
- Assemble the Oven and bake 10 minutes. Let stand 5 minutes.

Notes:

Marmalade-Almond Coffee Cake

In the first plastic bag, mix together:
* 1 cup all-purpose flour
* 3 tablespoons brown sugar
* ¼ cup white sugar
* ½ teaspoon baking powder
* ½ teaspoon baking soda
* 1/8 teaspoon salt

Carry separately:
* ½ cup orange marmalade
* 2 tablespoons sliced almonds
* 1 tablespoon vanilla extract
* 1 teaspoon almond extract

Preparation:
* Mix ½ cup water with the contents of the *first bag* in the Outback Oven pan.
* Stir in vanilla and almond extracts. Spread evenly over bottom of the Oven pan.
* Drop lumps of marmalade on top of the batter. Spread almonds on top.
* Assemble the Oven and bake 12 minutes. Let stand 5 minutes.

Notes:

Mince Bars

In the first plastic bag, mix together:
- 1¾ cup all-purpose baking mix
- ½ cup brown sugar
- 1 tablespoon dried egg
- ½ cup chopped nuts

Carry separately:
- 1 package condensed mincemeat (9 ounces)

Preparation:
- Mix ¾ cup water with the mincemeat in the Outback Oven pan.
- Set pan directly on stove and gently heat while breaking up the mincemeat block.
- When mincemeat is well blended, stir in the contents of the *first bag*.
- Add small amounts of water, if needed, to get a smooth batter.
- Assemble the Oven and bake 12 minutes. Let stand 5 minutes.

Notes:

Mint Meltaway Bars

In the first plastic bag, mix together:
- 1 package *Jiffy*® yellow cake mix (9 ounces; 1½ cups)
- 2 tablespoons non-dairy coffee creamer
- 1 tablespoon dry egg

Carry separately:
- ¾ cup miniature mints or similar small mint-flavored candies, crushed

Preparation:
- Mix ½ cup water with the contents of the *first bag* in the Outback Oven pan.
- Stir in mints.
- Assemble the Oven and bake 10 minutes. Let stand 5 minutes.

Notes:

Old-Fashioned Rice Pudding

In the first plastic bag, mix together:
- 1 cup instant rice
- 1 package vanilla or coconut cream pudding and pie filling (not instant)
- ¾ cup powdered milk
- ¼ cup non-dairy coffee creamer
- ¼ cup raisins
- 1 tablespoon dried egg
- ¼ teaspoon ground cinnamon
- 1/8 teaspoon ground nutmeg

Preparation:
- Mix 4 cups water with the contents of the *first bag* in a medium pan.
- Bring to a full boil stirring constantly. Reduce heat and simmer 3 minutes.
- Remove from heat and let stand 5 to 10 minutes.

Notes:

One-Pan Chocolate Chip Cookie

In the first plastic bag, mix together:
- 1 package *Jiffy*® yellow cake mix (9 ounces; 1½ cups)
- ½ cup chocolate chips (6 ounces)
- 1 tablespoon dried egg
- ¼ cup brown sugar, packed
- ¼ cup chopped nuts (optional)

Carry separately:
- 1 teaspoon vanilla extract

Preparation:
- Mix ½ cup water with the contents of the *first bag* in the Outback Oven pan.
- Stir in vanilla extract and mix until well blended.
- Assemble the Oven and bake 12 minutes. Let stand 5 minutes.

Notes:

Orange 'n Cream Drops

In the first plastic bag, mix together:
- 1½ cups all-purpose flour
- 1 cup sugar
- 1 tablespoon dry egg
- 1 teaspoon orange-flavored gelatin
- ½ teaspoon baking powder
- ½ teaspoon baking soda

Carry separately:
- 1 teaspoon vanilla extract
- ¼ cup white chocolate morsels

Preparation:
- Mix ¾ cup water with the contents of the *first bag* in the Outback Oven pan.
- Stir in vanilla and white chocolate morsels.
- Assemble the Oven and bake 12 minutes. Let stand 5 minutes.

Notes:

Orange Nut Squares

In the first plastic bag, mix together:
- 1½ cups carrot cake mix
- 3 tablespoons dry egg
- ¾ cup brown sugar, packed
- ¼ cup chopped nuts
- ½ teaspoon ground cinnamon

Carry separately:
- ½ cup orange marmalade
- ½ cup powdered sugar for topping (optional)

Preparation:
- Mix ¾ cup water with the contents of the *first bag* in the Outback Oven pan.
- Stir in marmalade and mix until well blended.
- Assemble the Oven and bake 12 minutes. Let stand 5 minutes.
- Shake powdered sugar on top.

Notes:

PB 'n Jam Bites

In the first plastic bag, mix together:
* 2½ cups rice cereal
* ¼ cup white sugar

Carry separately:
* ½ cup crunchy or smooth peanut butter
* ½ cup margarine
* ½ cup strawberry jam or preserves (not jelly)

Preparation:
* Mix the peanut butter, margarine and jam in a large pan.
* Heat gently, stirring constantly.
* When the mixture is liquid, quickly stir in the contents of the *first bag*.
* Mix well and spread over the bottom of the pan.
* Let stand to cool for 10 minutes.

Notes:

Peach and Cranberry Cobbler

In the first plastic bag, mix together:
- 1 cup dried peaches, chopped
- ½ cup dried cranberries
- ¾ cup white sugar
- ¼ teaspoon ground cinnamon (optional)

In the second plastic bag, mix together:
- 1 package cranberry muffin mix (7 ounces; 1¾ cups)

Preparation:
- Mix 1 cup water with the contents of the *first bag* in the Outback Oven pan.
- Set pan directly on the stove and bring to a boil.
- Reduce heat, cover and simmer 5 minutes.
- Remove from heat. Let stand 5 minutes.
- Pour ¾ cup water into the *second bag* and mix by squeezing the bag.
- Spread the batter over the fruit in the Oven pan.
- Assemble the Oven and bake 12 minutes. Let stand 5 minutes.

Notes:

Peanut Butter Cake

In the first plastic bag, mix together:
- 1 package *Jiffy*® yellow cake mix (9 ounces; 1½ cups)
- 1 tablespoon dried egg
- 2 tablespoons chopped peanuts or pecans

Carry separately:
- ¼ cup chunky or smooth peanut butter

Preparation:
- Mix ½ cup water with the contents of the *first bag* in the Outback Oven pan.
- Stir in peanut butter and mix until well blended.
- Assemble the Oven and bake 10 minutes. Let stand 5 minutes.

Notes:

Peanut Butter Chips and Jelly Bars

In the first plastic bag, mix together:
- 1½ cups all-purpose flour
- ½ cup white sugar
- ¾ teaspoon baking powder
- 2 tablespoons dried egg

Carry separately:
- ½ cup margarine
- ¾ cup grape jelly (or any other flavor)
- ¼ cup peanut butter chips candies

Preparation:
- Mix margarine with the contents of the *first bag* in the Outback Oven pan.
- With a knife, cut the margarine in until it's crumbly.
- Stir in ½ cup water until the batter is smooth.
- Remove ½ of the batter and spread the remainder across the bottom of the pan.
- Spread the jelly and chips on top and spread remaining batter on top.
- Assemble the Oven and bake 12 minutes. Let stand 5 minutes.

Notes:

Pecan Turtle Brownies

In the first plastic bag, mix together:
- 1 package *Jiffy*® brownie mix (8 ounces; 1¾ cups)
- 2 tablespoons powdered sugar
- 2 tablespoons dried egg

Carry separately:
- 1 tablespoon corn syrup mixed with ¼ teaspoon maple flavoring
- ½ cup chopped pecans or 12-18 whole pecans

Preparation:
- Mix ½ cup water with the contents of the *first bag* in the Outback Oven pan.
- Stir in corn syrup and spread evenly in the pan. Sprinkle pecans on top.
- Assemble the Oven and bake 10 minutes. Let stand 5 minutes.

Notes:

Pudding Cake

In the first plastic bag, mix together:
- 1 package *Jiffy*® yellow cake mix (8 ounces; 1¾ cups)
- 1 package instant vanilla pudding mix (3.9 ounces)
- 3 tablespoons powdered milk
- 1 tablespoon non-dairy coffee creamer
- 4 tablespoons dried egg
- ¼ cup chopped nuts or fruit (optional)

Preparation:
- Mix ¾ cup water with the contents of the *first bag* in the Outback Oven pan.
- Stir until all lumps are gone.
- Assemble the Oven and bake 10 minutes.
- Let stand 5 to 10 minutes before serving.

Notes:

Raspberry Bars

In the first plastic bag, mix together:
- 1 package *Jiffy*® raspberry-flavored muffin mix (8 ounces; 1¾ cups)
- 2 tablespoons dried egg
- ¼ cup quick cooking oats
- ¼ cup chopped nuts

Carry separately:
- ¼ cup raspberry jam or preserves (not jelly)

Preparation:
- Mix ½ cup water with the contents of the *first bag* in the Outback Oven pan.
- Stir in raspberry jam or preserves.
- Add small amounts of water to make a thick smooth batter.
- Assemble the Oven and bake 12 minutes.

Notes:

Raspberry-Strawberry Cake

In the first plastic bag, mix together:
- 1 package *Jiffy*® raspberry muffin mix (8 ounces, 1½ cups)
- 2 tablespoons dried egg
- 2 tablespoons vanilla instant pudding mix
- ¼ cup powdered milk
- ½ teaspoon almond extract
- 2 tablespoons chopped pecans

Carry separately:
- ½ cup strawberry jam or preserves

Preparation:
- Mix ¾ cup water with the contents of the *first bag* in the Outback Oven pan.
- Stir in strawberry preserves.
- Assemble the Oven and bake 12 minutes. Let stand 5 minutes.

Notes:

Rice Peach Melba

In the first plastic bag, mix together:
- 1 cup dried peaches, chopped
- ¼ cup powdered milk
- 2 tablespoons non-dairy coffee creamer

In the second plastic bag, mix together:
- ¾ cup instant rice
- ¼ cup sugar
- ½ teaspoon salt
- 1/8 teaspoon nutmeg

Preparation:
- Mix 2¼ cups water with the contents of the *first bag* in a medium pan.
- Bring to a boil, reduce heat, cover and simmer 8-10 minutes.
- Remove from heat and stir in the contents of the *second bag*.
- Mix well cover and let stand 5 to 10 minutes.

Notes:

Sugar and Almond Pastry

In the first plastic bag, mix together:
- 1¾ cups all-purpose baking mix
- ¼ cup sugar

In the second plastic bag, mix together:
- ½ cup brown sugar
- ¼ cup slivered almonds
- ¼ teaspoon ground cinnamon

Carry separately:
- ½ cup powdered sugar
- 2 teaspoons almond extract

Preparation:
- Mix ¾ cup water with the contents of the *first bag* in the Outback Oven pan.
- Stir in almond extract and spread over the bottom of the pan.
- Shake the *second bag* until sugar and nuts are well blended.
- Spread evenly over the top of the batter in the Oven pan.
- Assemble the Oven and bake 10 minutes.
- Mix 2 teaspoons water with powdered sugar and drizzle over the pastry.

Notes:

Vanilla Raspberry Loaf

In the first plastic bag, mix together:
- 1 package *Jiffy*® raspberry muffin mix (8 ounces; 1¾ cup)
- 1 tablespoon instant vanilla pudding
- 2 tablespoons dried egg
- 2 tablespoons quick cooking oats

Preparation:
- Mix ¾ cup water with the contents of the *first bag* in the Outback Oven pan.
- Stir until well blended.
- Assemble the Oven and bake 10 minutes. Let stand 3 minutes.

Notes:

Welsh Tea Loaf

In the first plastic bag, mix together:
- 1½ cups all-purpose flour
- ¾ cup sugar
- ½ cup raisins
- ¼ cup powdered milk
- 2 tablespoons dried egg
- 2 teaspoons baking soda
- Pinch of salt

Carry separately:
- 2 teaspoons vanilla
- 1 tablespoon molasses

Preparation:
- Mix ¾ cup water with the contents of the *first bag* in the Outback Oven pan.
- Stir in vanilla and molasses.
- Assemble the Oven and bake 12 minutes. Let stand 5 minutes.

Notes:

-Five-

Leave No Trace and Lightweight Cooking

"Waste is worse than loss. The time is coming when every person who lays claim to ability will keep the question of waste before him constantly. The scope of thrift is limitless."

Thomas A. Edison

When I started backpacking almost 30 years ago, many wilderness campers practiced the three B's of wilderness cleanup: Burn, Bash and Bury*. Burn anything that is remotely flammable including foil lined food packets, Bash everything else flat with a rock and Bury the whole mess in a campfire circle made from fist-sized rocks. Fortunately, this process is being replaced with the three R's: Recycle, Reuse and Reduce. Recycle everything possible, Reuse containers and packaging and Reduce the amount of materials used and carried into remote areas. Then carry it back out. Central to the three R's are the principles of Leave No Trace camping.

Leave No Trace (LNT) is a non-profit organization that has been promoting low-impact backcountry travel for almost a decade*. The mission of LNT is "to promote and inspire responsible outdoor recreation through education, research and partnerships." LNT is a lot more than a campaign for clean trails and campsites, however. LNT literature describes it as a

---

* A certain national youth group was notorious for this practice. Although they have recently adopted Leave No Trace principles, their most recent handbook still recommends that campers "burn [leftover food] in a hot campfire" and that they "can burn wastepaper too." Still, I guess some progress is being made.

* Leave No Trace can be found on the Internet at www.lnt.org or at 800-332-4100.

"program dedicated to building awareness, appreciation and most of all, respect for our public recreation places. LNT is about enjoying the great outdoors while traveling and camping with care."

At the core of the LNT philosophy are seven principles that should be used to guide all outdoor activities.

- **Plan ahead and prepare**
- **Travel and camp on durable surfaces**
- **Dispose of waste properly**
- **Leave what you find**
- **Minimize campfire impacts**
- **Respect wildlife**
- **Be considerate of other visitors**

In a world of increasing pressure on finite natural resources, every wilderness chef has an obligation to recognize the impact of his or her activities on the natural world and must work to minimize that impact. Learn these principles of Leave No Trace camping and how they apply specifically to wilderness cooking. Practice LNT. Tread gently on the earth and with each step, savor the smallest part of the total experience.

"May all your trails be crooked, winding, lonesome, dangerous, leading to the most amazing view…where something strange and more beautiful and more full of wonder than your deepest dreams waits for you."

Edward Abbey

-Six-

The Last Words

"The secret of good cooking resides in the cook's ability to say 'the hell with the basic recipe' and improvise freely from it. If you haven't got this kind of moxie, you might as well hang up your apron."

James Alan McPherson

If you have favorite new recipes you have discovered or some 'moxie' variations on recipes in this book you would like to share, send them to:

John Weber
313 8th St. NW
Mount Vernon, Iowa 52314
Email: JWEBER @CORNELLCOLLEGE.EDU

They will be included in the next edition with appropriate credit. If there is a humorous anecdote or story to go with the recipe, include it also. In the meantime, I wish everyone:

"…Bon Appetite (literal translation: 'Chow Down')."

Dave Barry[*]

---

[*] I gleaned the quotations from a lot of sources. Sadly, I had to leave out some exquisitely acerbic statements about cooking and food from some well-known curmudgeons such as W. C. Fields because of the comment's lack of taste.

Appendix I

Other Cookbooks

The following is bibliography of outdoor cookbooks. Most of them are oriented toward lightweight cooking for backpackers, hikers and paddlers. Some are excellent but others make me wonder what the author's definition of "lightweight" is. (Do backpackers really carry containers of dry white wine?) All were in print at the time of this writing and can be found at the online bookstores listed at the end of **Appendix II**.

Adare, Sierra: *Backcountry Cooking*, Tamarack Books, Inc.
Axcell, Claudia & Diana Cooke: *Simple Foods for the Pack*, Sierra Club Books
Barker, Harriett: *The One-Burner Gourmet*, Contemporary Books
Bates, Dorothy R.: *The TVP Cookbook*, The Book Publishing Company
Brunell, Valerie & Ralph Swain: *Wilderness Ranger Cookbook*, Falcon Press
Capossela, Jim: *Camp & Trail Cooking Techniques*, The Countryman Press
Fleming, June: *The Well-Fed Backpacker*, Vintage Books
Gray, Melissa & Buck Tildon: *Cooking the One Burner Way*, ICS Books
Gunn, Carolyn: *Trail Food: Easy, Healthy & Delicious*, Rodale Press, Inc.
Hunter, Gerald R. & Peggy Hoffmann: *Bake a Snake, How to Survive by Your Own Cooking*, Meridional Publications
Jacobson, Cliff: *The Basic Essentials of Cooking in the Outdoors*, ICS Books
Jacobson, Don & Don Mauer: *The One Pan Gourmet Cooks Lite*, ICS Books
Kreissman, Bern: *Eating Hearty in the Wilderness with Absolutely No Cleanup*, Bear Klaw Press
Kesselheim, Alan S.: *The Lightweight Gourmet*, Ragged Mountain Press
Kesselheim, Alan S.: *Trail Food*, Ragged Mountain Press

271

Latimer, Carole: *Wilderness Cuisine*, Wilderness Press

Logue, Frank and Victoria: *Cooking for Campers and Backpackers*, Menasha Ridge Press

Marrone, Teresa: *The Back-Country Kitchen*, Northern Trails Press

McHugh, Gretchen: *The Hungry Hiker's Book of Good Cooking*, Knopf, Inc.

McMorris, Bill & Jo: *Camp Cooking*, Lyons and Burford

Miller, Dorcas S.: *Good Food for Camp and Trail*, Pruett Publishing

Miller, Dorcas S.: *Backcountry Cooking*, The Mountaineers

O'Keefe, M. Timothy: *The Spicy Camp Cookbook*, Menasha Ridge Press

Prater, Yvonne & Ruth Dyar Mendenhall: *Gorp, Glop & Glue Stew*, The Mountaineers

Ragsdale, John: *Camper's Guide to Outdoor Cooking*, Gulf Publishing

Spangenburg, Jean S.: *The Backpacker's Companion*, Sylva Herald Publishing

Spangenburg, Jean and Samuel: *The Portable Baker*, Ragged Mountain Press

Sukey, Richard: *NOLS Cookery*, Stackpole Books

Thomas, Dian: *Roughing It Easy*, Dian Thomas Company

Viehman, John: *Trailside's Trail Food*, Rodale Press

Wallace, Aubrey: *Natural Foods for the Trail*, Vogelsang Press

Weber, John R.: *The Wilderness Chef, The Art and Craft of Lightweight Cooking*, iUniverse Press

White, Linda: *Cooking on a Stick*, Campfire Recipes for Kids, Gibbs-Smith

Yaffe, Linda Frederick: *High Trail Cookery*, Chicago Review Press

Appendix II

Internet Resources

The Internet is a cornucopia of resources for any cook. Most of the major food manufacturers have home pages with cooking tips, tutorials, product information, nutritional data and thousands of recipes, many of which can be adapted to outdoor preparation with just a little imagination. You can even sign up to receive recipes automatically via e-mail. Some sites aren't particularly useful* for outdoor camp cooking but I included them for no other reason than they're fun to visit.

For those who may not be familiar with the idiosyncratic nature of web pages, keep in mind that web pages come and go rapidly, especially if the organization or business is small. At the time this was written, all links were working. However, when you try them weeks or months later, they may be gone.

Absolutely the best site to visit for recipes and just about anything even remotely connected with cooking is: **www.cdkitchen.com**. The site boasts more than 200,000 recipes. Having spent many hours there, I can readily believe the claim. Another site with a collection of more than 70,000 recipes is: **www.recipesource.com**. There is also a collection of more than 1 million (1,094,579 recipes to be exact) on a CD from *ARC International* titled "Easy Chef's One Million of the World's Best Recipes." It's available at discount stores in the "housewares" section.

---

* The Hostess Twinkie site with "Captain Cupcake" and the "Ding Dong Kingdom" (seriously!) may a bit over the top for lightweight cooking, but people have different tastes.

Here are some other web pages by food manufacturers and distributors I have found useful or just entertaining:

- American Beauty Pasta: www.nwpasta.com/beauty
- American Dairy Association: www.ilovecheese.com
- American Italian Pasta Company: www.pastalabella
- Arm & Hammer Cookbook: www.armhammer.com
- Armour Swift-Eckrich: www.ase-dsd.com
- At Home On The Range: www.hotrange.com
- Azteca Foods: www.aztecafoods.com
- Better Homes And Gardens: www.bhglive.com/food/index.html
- Betty Crocker: www.bettycrocker.com
- Bird's Eye: www.birdseye.com
- Bisquick Baking Mix: www.bisquick.com
- Bumble Bee Seafood: www.bumblebee.com
- Butterball Turkey: www.butterball.com
- Campbell Soup: www.campbellsoup.com
- Cannon Foods: www.cannon.com.au
- Chex Cereal: www.wish-bone.com
- Chicken Of The Sea: www.chickenofthesea.com
- Cloverdale Foods Pork Products: www.cloverdalefoods.com
- Compucook Online Resource For Food And Cooking: www.compucook.com
- Crisco: www.criscokitchen.com/recipes01.html
- Delmonte: www.delmonte.com
- Dole Foods: www.dole.com
- Dominick's Food Stores: www.dominicks.com
- Duncan Hines: www.duncanhines.com
- Eagle Brand Condensed Milk: www.eaglebrand.com
- Epicurious Gourmet: www.gourmet.com
- Egg Board: www.aeb.org
- Farmland Foods Prepared Meats: www.farmlandfood.com
- Fleischmann's Baking: www.breadworld.com

- Frito-Lay: www.fritolay.com
- General Mills: www.genmills.com
- General Mills' Betty Crocker Cookbook Pages: www.bettycrocker.com
- Godiva Chocolate: www.godiva.com
- Gorton's Fisherman's Cookbook: www.gortons.com
- Green Giant: www.greengiant.com
- I Can't Believe It's Not Butter: www.tasteyoulove.com
- Idaho Potatoes: www.idahopotatoes.com
- Jolly Time Popcorn: www.jollytime.com
- Hellmann's Diner: www.hellmanns.ca
- Hershey's Chocolate: www.hersheys.com
- Hidden Valley Ranch Recipes: www.hiddenvalley.com
- Home Baking Association: www.homebaking.org
- Hormel Foods: www.hormel.com
- Hostess Recipes: www.twinkies.com
- Hot Dog And Sausage Council: www.hot-dog.org
- Hulman Baking Powder Recipes: www.hulman.com
- Hunts Tomato Expert Site: www.hunts.com
- HyVee Food Stores: www.hy-vee.com
- Jelly Belly Jelly Beans: www.jellybelly.com
- Jiffy Mixes: www.jiffymix.com
- Kellogg's: www.kelloggs.com
- King Arthur Flour: www.kingarthurflour.com
- Kraft Foods: www.kraftfoods.com
- Land O' Lakes Butter Recipes: www.landolakes.com
- Louis Kemp Seafood Recipes: www.louiskemp.com
- Lipton: www.recipesecrets.com
- McCormick spices: www.mccormick.com
- Millstone Coffee: www.millstone.com
- Mission Foods Tortillas: www.missionfoods.com
- Mott's Applesauce Recipes: www.motts.com
- Nabisco: www.nabisco.com

- Nestle's: www.nestle.com
- Nestle's Baking Recipes: www.verybestbaking.com
- Norbest Turkey: www.norbest.com
- Ortega Mexican Recipes: www.ortega.com
- Ore-Ida Potatoes: www.ore-ida.com
- Oscar Mayer: www.kraftfoods.com/oscar-mayer
- Pastry Wiz: www.pastrywiz.com
- Pie Recipes: www.pierecipe.com
- Pillsbury: www.pillsbury.com/main/brands/dessert.html
- Pillsbury Bakeoff Recipes: www.bakeoff.com/
- Popcorn Recipes And Other Snacks: www.popcorn.org/mpindex.htm
- Quaker Oats: www.quakeroats.com
- Quaker Oatmeal: www.quakeroatmeal.com
- Ragu Sauces Recipes: www.eat.com
- ReaLemon & ReaLime: www.realemon.com
- Recipes For Just About Anything: www.allrecipes.com
- Reynolds Kitchen: www2.rmc.com/reynoldskitchens/kitchen-connection
- Rice-A-Roni: www.ricearoni.com
- Robin Hood Flour: www.robinhood.ca/
- Rocky Mountain Survival Group: www.artrans.com/rmsg/cook/recipes.htm
- Safeway Food Stores: www.safeway.com
- Sargento Cheese: www.sargento.com
- Site For Public Posting Of Recipes: www.my-recipe.com
- Smuckers: www.smucker.com
- Sue Bee Honey: www.suebee.com
- Success Rice: www.successrice.com
- Sun Maid Raisins: www.sun-maid.com
- Starkist: www.starkist.com
- Sunkist: www.sunkist.com
- Swanson Broth Recipes: www.swansonbroth.com

- Tabasco Sauce: www.tabasco.com
- Taste Of Home:
  www.tasteofhome.com/Recipes/RecipeIndex.html
- Tyson's Foods: www.tyson.com
- Uncle Ben's Rice: www.unclebens.com
- Wegman's Food Markets: www.wegmans.com
- Wild Oats: www.wildoats.com
- Wish-bone Salad Dressing: www.wish-bone.com

For more information about Leave No Trace camping:

- www.lnt.org

Food Safety:

- www.foodsafety.org
- www.ces.ncsu.edu/depts/foodsci/agentinfo/

Other web pages that may be of interest:

- Cook's Thesaurus: http://www.switcheroo.com
  Everything anyone would need to know about a cooking terms or techniques.

- E-Zines: www.cdkitchen.com/links/Z/E-Zines
  Online electronic magazines with just about anything imaginable (and some things that I couldn't imagine) about food, cooking, recipes, etc.

- GORP, Great Outdoor Recreation Pages: www.gorp.com
  A huge collection of outdoor and wilderness information including food, travel, activities, gear selection and books.

- The Nissin Ramen Page: **www.nissinfoods.com**
  These recipes aren't particularly suited for outdoor preparation, but you may want to whip one up at home.

- The Official Ramen Homepage: **www.umr.edu/~sbrondel/ramen.html**
  More than 160 Ramen noodle recipes including anecdotes and stories about the recipe that make the page worth a visit just for the humor.

- TSR Recipes: **www.topsecretrecipes.com/recipes.htm**
  Recipes of famous brand-name foods (McDonald's secret sauce, Girl Scout cookies, etc.) that can be prepared at home.

Online bookstores:

Additional titles of cookbooks, camping, backpacking, canoeing or just about any other subject, can be found at Amazon Books, Barnes and Noble, or Borders bookstores online:

Amazon Books: **www.amazon.com**
Barnes and Noble: **www.barnsandnoble.com**
Borders Books: **www.borders.com**

To find cookbooks on lightweight camping at these sites, perform a search on the string: "Outdoor Cookery." Be prepared to wade through a *huge* number of grilling and outdoor barbecuing cookbooks to find a handful of backpacking/camping cookbooks though. If the number of books on these subjects is any indication of the number of people grilling in the backyard, I'm surprised there isn't a charcoal shortage.

Appendix III

Backpacking/Wilderness Resources

Getchell, Annie: *The Essential Outdoor Gear Manual,* Ragged Mountain Press
Manning, Harvey: *Backpacking One Step at a Time*, Vintage Books
McGivney, Annette: *Leave No Trace*, The Mountaineers
Schad, Jerry & David S. Moser: *Wilderness Basics, The Complete Handbook for Hikers & Backpackers,* The Mountaineers
Townsend, Chris: *The Backpacker's Handbook*, Ragged Mountain Press

Equipment Sources:

Outback Oven is available from Campmor and REI, listed below.

Prepackaged food sources that carry premixed meals for the Outback Oven include:

The Campers Pantry
PO Box 293
Farmington, MN 55024-0293
(612) 463-3765
www.alcasoft.com:80/campers-pantry/

Adventure Foods
125 Deer Forest Rd.
Fayetteville, GA 30214
1-888-241-1864
www.ewalker.com/adgear/foodady.htm

General Camping/Outdoor Equipment

Recreation Equipment Incorporated
Sumner, WA 98352-0001
(800) 426-4840
www.rei.com

Campmor
(800) 226-7667
www.campmor.com

TVP Sources

The Mail Order Catalog for Healthy Eating
Box 180
Summertown, TN 38483
931-964-2241
www.healthy-eating.com

Patricia Stirm's Way West Enterprises
31776 Hwy. 41 Coarsegold, CA 93614
(209) 683-6993
www.slip.net/~dmd/pswaywest.shtml

Other Resources:

The Baker's Catalog is a great source of baking tools, flours and spices of all kinds. Most are not applicable for outdoor cooking, but would be of interest to anyone who likes to cook. Of interest to the outdoor chef are dried fruits, hard-to-find dried seasonings, dried and powdered vegetables such as red and green peppers, dried dairy products such as dried cheeses and sour cream, nuts, dried egg and much more. A ½ pound package of these items goes a long way—try it; you'll like it. The web site has an online catalog, but it's not as complete as the printed catalog.

The Baker's Catalog
King Arthur Flour
PO Box 876
Norwich, VT 05055-9900
www.kingarthurflour.com

Appendix IV

Metric Conversion Chart

Volume Measurements (Dry)
1/8 teaspoon = 0.5 ml
¼ teaspoon = 1 ml
½ teaspoon = 2 ml
¾ teaspoon = 4 ml
1 teaspoon = 5 ml
1 tablespoon = 15 ml
¼ cup = 60 ml
½ cup = 75 ml
¾ cup = 175 ml
1 cup = 250 ml
2 cups = 1 pint = 500 ml

Weights (Mass)
½ ounce = 15 g
1 ounce = 30 g
4 ounces = 120 g
8 ounces = 225 g
12 ounces = 360 g
16 ounces = 1 pound = 450 g

Index

52

About the Author

John Weber has camped, backpacked, canoed, kayaked and cooked (!) in many of this country's wild places in the last 30 years. Along the way, he has prepared, developed and collected many 1000's of recipes that he shares with fellow travelers in his Wilderness Chef series of cookbooks.

0-595-21505-X

Printed in the United Kingdom
by Lightning Source UK Ltd.
104066UKS00001B/283